More Good Food
for good friends

by dirk hoffius

First Edition

Copyright © 2023 by Dirk C. Hoffius

All rights reserved. No part of this publication may be reproduced or transmitted in any form by any means, except brief excerpts for the purpose of review, without written permission of the author.

Cover photo courtesy of the Grand Rapids Community Foundation.

Published in the United States

Printed by Sheridan Saline, Inc., Saline, MI

ISBN: 979-8-218-27031-5

Table of Contents

Introduction v
Getting Started - The Basics vii
Appetizers 1
Salads 21
Soups 29
Vegetables 39
Side Dishes 47
Salts & Sauces 53
Beef, Pork, & Lamb 63
Poultry 75
Seafood 83
Pasta / Italian 93
Brunch 101
Bread & Sandwiches 113
Desserts 125
Acknowledgments 141
Index 143

Grant,
This is a nice basic cookbook written by our friend. Enjoy

Introduction

Unbelievably, this is my second cookbook. The first, *Just Good Food for good friends*, was printed in 2009. I had become frustrated with recipes in cookbooks that called for ingredients that I'd never heard of or couldn't easily locate. It was one of those projects that started innocently enough, with recipes written in pencil in a three-ring binder. I started telling friends what I was doing and shared some of the recipes for input. As the recipes were made again and again, they were tweaked and improved along the way. Next I was being asked when I planned to publish and what was my theme? I would moan and say that I didn't have a theme, the recipes are just good food. Result: a theme!

I published in late December of 2009 and missed the holiday season. Oops! I ordered two thousand copies and thought my estate would have plenty to give away at my funeral. Instead, they were gone by July of 2010. By now I have had a total of five thousand printed. Amazon? Never! All were sold personally or by West Michigan sites that know me. Two bear special mention: Mason Jones, formerly known as Papers Plus, and the Meijer Gardens Holiday Show and Gift Shop.

One of the "opportunities" I had not prepared for was being auctioned off to prepare a meal using recipes in the cookbook. Clearly, I needed help and Marilyn Lankfer and Karen Maczugo in my office offered to serve as sous-chefs. My top assistants, my only assistants, my partners in each of these projects. Most importantly, they made each dinner special for the guests and for us.

Why a second cookbook? Friends started asking if I was working on another one. I had written down many new recipes, but still had some work to do. I wanted to complement the recipes in *Just Good Food* without repeating any. After more input, tweaking, and improving, I'm excited to share with you *More Good Food for good friends*. I hope you find a recipe in here that becomes a favorite that you can share with your good friends.

In the first cookbook I included recipes for several spice collections, which you could make for yourself or in larger quantities, to share with friends. Lots of people took advantage of those so I'm including them again in this book, but even more asked how they could buy those spices. So in 2015 I finally made several of them—Thyme for Salt, Rattlesnake Salt, and Tuscan Rosemary Salt—available for sale. And later the Savory Grilling Rub, too. So if you buy the jars, you won't have to make them yourself. If you'd like to buy a jar (or several), you might go to Dirksgoodseasonings.com and place an order. Or, if you're near Grand Rapids, Michigan (and who isn't?), you could go buy some from my friends at:

- Mason Jones, 1862 Breton Road SE;
- Art of the Table, 606 Wealthy Street SE; and
- Frederick Meijer Gardens & Sculpture Park Gift Shop, 1000 East Beltline Avenue NE.

Dirk

Getting Started — The Basics

Preparation
First, make sure you have all of the ingredients. Many of these recipes were selected because they use things we typically have on hand. When you start a recipe, gather the ingredients in the proper amounts so that when the dish is complete everything is gone. You should also read through the entire recipe to note the order of assembly. Often times a group of ingredients are to be combined before mixing with others.

Washing, Peeling, and Trimming
Vegetables, meat, and seafood should be washed and dried with paper towels just before cooking. Use lukewarm water to wash away dirt, pesticides, bacteria, fungi, and the byproducts of handling. The objective is to trim off what you don't want to cook, whether it's fat, a bad spot, a bruise, or skin.

You will note I did not include poultry for washing, which I had done in *Just Good Food*. There is some dispute, but I think the conclusion is that heating the chicken to 165° will kill the dreaded salmonella and campylobacter bacteria. Washing chicken risks spreading the bacteria on the counter, cutting board, and more.

Clean-Up
One of the most difficult lessons to learn is cleaning up as you go. Of course, having an assistant to help clean up is a gift, a true partnership in the cooking experience. The time you spend cleaning pans and work surfaces after you finish each step will reward you in time saved and efficiency as you continue. Try to make it a habit. No matter who does the cleaning, Bar Keepers Friend and Cascade powder are very helpful. Dissolve a little of either in a pan or baking dish that you're having trouble cleaning. Leave it for 20 minutes or overnight and clean-up should be a breeze! But for ease of cleanup, try Dawn Ultra Platinum Powerwash dish spray. Then wipe, rinse, and dry.

Butter and Oil
Yes, butter. You will find it mentioned often. Don't get carried away with it, but enjoy what it does to your food. We now know it is healthier (in moderation) than the fats we thought were going to save us.

Throughout this book I refer to extra virgin olive oil. That means the first cold pressing of the olive. The taste may vary slightly with each bottle, but it is an oil that has a distinct flavor that reminds you of its source. It has a lower smoke point than canola oil and has more flavor than canola oil. For an even higher smoke point and also heart healthy, try adding avocado oil to your repertoire. All in all, a little research may help you find the perfect oil for your next cooking adventure.

Cookie Tips
Cookies are one of those simple foods that will win you friends. There are some things you can do to assure a better result. First, your ingredients should be at room temperature, especially eggs and butter. Cold eggs and cold butter do not mix well and melted butter is even worse. You will normally cream the butter in the sugar and then add one egg at a time, beating or whipping the mixture so that there is a lot of air, thereby producing lighter cookies. Finally, stir by hand or beat slowly when you add the flour as over-beating the flour results in hard cookies. So you whip the butter, sugar, and eggs, but stir in the flour.

Knives
Surprisingly, you are less likely to cut yourself with a sharp knife than with a dull one. Maintain your knives and keep them sharp. It should reduce the preparation time as well. It may also avoid tears when you cut an onion. You want an 8-inch knife as your basic knife (10-inch for big hands and 6-inch for small hands). You should also have a paring knife and a long serrated bread knife; everything else is icing on the cake. Quality knives should not be put through the dishwasher as it dulls them. Learn to sharpen your knives with a sharpening steel or a diamond-hone sharpener with different stages to do a rough and then a fine sharpening.

Pots and pans
You will find references to the cast-iron pan you may have thrown away years ago. I feel for you. I bought one when I went to law school and I still have it. Like a good friend, it stays loyal and true. Cast-iron pans are better for searing, and you can put them in the oven to finish the dish like a real chef. Works great for pork tenderloin, steak, fish, and more. I also have at least one stainless-steel pan for the same reason: You can sear and move straight into the oven. For everyday cooking, high-quality nonstick pans are best. The technology keeps changing, so it's worth doing some research to make sure you have the best and safest.

I also favor Pyrex, porcelain, and ceramic pie and baking dishes. However, I often find myself reaching for a metal pan and some aluminum foil to make clean-up easier.

Salt and Spices
I specify kosher salt to provide consistency. I avoid sea salts because they have a variety of minerals that can affect the taste of a dish. We grew up on Morton's salt with iodine. Unfortunately, it is twice as salty as kosher salt. As a result, I now specify kosher salt; coarse is preferred but fine can be used for baking. The coarser the salt, the less you need because it is saltier.

I also specify coarse-ground black pepper; freshly ground would be the best but it is hard to measure. So it is up to you: grind it fresh and estimate the amount or use pre-ground and get the quantity perfect but sacrifice some of the taste. When I'm cooking I err on the side of less salt and pepper because you can always taste at the end and add more if needed.

It is worthwhile to evaluate and replace spices you have had in the cabinet for many years. It does make a difference, especially when you can do it at a reasonable cost from a company like Penzeys Spices (penzeys.com).

Appetizers

Charleston Cheese

serves one party

12 ounces extra-sharp cheddar cheese, grated
4 ounces (½ cup) Samuel Adams Lager or Two Hearted Ale (or your favorite)
Juice 1 lemon (2-3 tablespoons), strained
2 tablespoons ketchup
2 tablespoons Worcestershire sauce
1 tablespoon prepared horseradish
2 teaspoons hot sauce, such as Tabasco or Frank's
2 teaspoons Dijon mustard
1 clove garlic, minced

Combine all of the ingredients in a food processor and pulse until the mixture is smooth. Remove the mixture and put in a bowl and refrigerate until ready to serve. This can be made ahead and a few extra days won't hurt.

Of course, it is great on crostini, crackers, and fresh vegetables.

A cheese very much like this was popular in restaurants in Charleston, S.C. in the 1950s and '60s, but it might be even better when made at home.

The bonus to this recipe is the remaining beer. Wait, you drank it already?!

Cheese Straws

serves 8-12

8 ounces extra-sharp white cheddar cheese, grated
1 stick butter, softened and cut into pieces
1½ cups all-purpose flour, plus more for dusting the board
1 teaspoon kosher salt
¼ teaspoon cayenne pepper
2 tablespoons cream (or half and half, milk, or water)

Put the cheese, butter, flour, salt, and pepper in a food processor and pulse until the mixture resembles coarse crumbs. Add the liquid and process until a ball is formed, adding a little more liquid if necessary to form the ball. You may find it best to split into 2 balls.

Dust a board with flour and place the cheese ball on the surface. Flatten the ball, dust it with flour, and roll the dough into a rectangle about ⅛ – ¼ inch thick. Cut the dough with a sharp knife, cleaning as necessary, into long strips about ¼ inch wide. Some strips may be longer than others, it won't matter as you will enjoy them whatever the length, and really long strips are prone to break into small ones anyway!

Gently transfer the cheese strips to un-greased cookie sheet(s) with a space between each strip so that each strip can brown. Bake in a preheated 350° oven 12–15 minutes until slightly browned, turning halfway through. Cool and enjoy!

Cheese straws are a great appetizer and are readily available in stores. Guess when they were created? Hint, read the list of ingredients.

The biggest problem with these is making sure there are enough for the party. Something seems to happen between baking and serving. They are way too easy to pick up and eat as you walk by.

If half of the recipe is enough, you can turn the other half into a log covered with waxed paper and stored in the refrigerator in a plastic bag. You can later slice the log and bake the wafers or allow to warm slightly and turn into a ball and complete as cheese straws.

Cheese Puffs
serves one small party

Sliced white sandwich bread ½ inch thick (1 loaf is more than enough)
8 ounces cream cheese, softened
¼ cup grated Parmesan cheese
1 teaspoon onion powder

Preheat the oven to 350°. Using a 1-inch mold, cut 5 rings from each slice of bread, avoiding the crust. Place the rings on a parchment paper-lined sheet tray. Toast in the oven for 5 minutes or so until the rings are golden. Remove from the oven and let the trays cool.

Add the remaining ingredients to a food processor, pulse until thoroughly blended. Place the cheese mixture in a piping bag with a star tip or smooth flute and pipe a rosette of cheese on each ring.

Place under the broiler (not too close) 2–3 minutes until golden and serve immediately. As you can see, the toasted bread rounds can be made ahead along with the cheese mixture. Then wait for your guests to have a drink, and pipe the cheese and broil. This can be the only appetizer for the night.

Most of this recipe can be prepared ahead of time. Like so many things in life, preparation is key. Have a plan and stick to it.

Having an assistant is nice, like the friend that is always offering to help and you keep saying no. Say yes this time, it's more fun with an accomplice.

In Just Good Food I *included a cheese puff recipe with cheddar cheese. This is a great alternative using cream cheese. It's a good recipe to pass at the beginning of a cocktail party as they come out of the oven.*

Blue Cheese Dip
serves one party

16 ounces (1 pound) cream cheese, softened
2 tablespoons grated onion with its juice
3–4 ounces Roquefort or blue cheese, crumbled

Combine all of the ingredients in a food processor and pulse until the mixture is smooth.

Remove the mixture from the food processor and put in a bowl and refrigerate until ready to serve. This should be made ahead so that the flavors blend and set in. Go ahead, sample it to be sure it's good for your party, but not too much.

It is great on crostini, crackers, pretzels, and fresh vegetables, especially carrots, celery, and sliced green or red peppers.

This can be made with less onion and less blue cheese if you find it is too flavorful. In other words, less may be more for you. June agrees and she calls the less is more recipe "Bowman Dip."

We are all used to blue cheese sauces with sour cream, Greek yogurt, and/or mayonnaise. They are easy to spill on your shirt or skirt, but not this one! It still has great flavor, and it is so simple to make. An easy dip to take to a party!

Cajun Dip
serves one party

1 cup sour cream (or Greek yogurt or a combination of the two)
2 garlic cloves, chopped fine or minced
2 teaspoons tomato paste
1 jalapeno pepper, seeded and chopped fine
Kosher salt and coarse ground pepper, a dash of each, then adjust

Mix all of the ingredients in a bowl and refrigerate until ready to serve with cut vegetables (carrots, celery, red or green peppers), crackers, or chips.

Blue cheese alternative:
The Blue Cheese Dip uses cream cheese to avoid the problem of spilling it all over. If you substitute blue cheese for the tomato paste and omit or minimize the garlic and jalapeno pepper, you have another blue cheese dip.

Queso Dip:
Cut up 16 ounces of Velveeta cheese in a double boiler with water just touching the bottom of the pan. Heat and add 1 can Ro-Tel original diced tomatoes and green chillies. Stir until the cheese is melted and the Ro-Tel is combined. Serve with your favorite corn chips, using plates and small bowls to minimize dripping and double dipping.

This is a quick dip you can whip up in a matter of minutes.

A tube of tomato paste is the answer for the 2 teaspoons. Good to have some on hand for thickening other tomato dishes like a marinara or chili.

The Queso Dip is not a normal recipe for me, but in a quarantine it was a quick solution to the question of what to eat?

Curry Dip
serves 2 parties!

1 cup sour cream or Greek yogurt
1 cup mayonnaise
2 tablespoons cider vinegar
2 tablespoons sugar
2 teaspoons curry powder
2 teaspoons prepared horseradish, drained
2 teaspoons grated onion
1 teaspoon garlic powder

Mix the sour cream, mayonnaise, and vinegar. Then mix the remaining ingredients and add them to the wet ingredients, stirring to combine.

Chill several hours before serving with fresh vegetables and even chips.

Another dip to get you out of a jam. Again, it's all things you are likely to have on hand. And it's a different flavor for fresh vegetables for your friends who want to stay healthy. They will hardly eat enough dip to matter so you'll have plenty left over for party number two!

Hummus with Thyme
serves 12-16

2 cans (15 ounces each) garbanzo beans or chickpeas, drained, with liquid reserved
½ cup tahini (sesame-seed paste)
4–5 garlic cloves, peeled and chopped
Juice of 2 lemons, including 1 teaspoon lemon zest
1 tablespoon dried thyme or 2 tablespoons fresh thyme, chopped
2–4 tablespoons of the reserved bean liquid
1½ teaspoons kosher salt
1 teaspoon ancho chili, dried, or 10 dashes Tobasco, more or less

Put the beans in the food processor with the remaining ingredients on the top. Process until smooth and adjust the seasonings to taste. It may take a bit of processing and the 2–4 tablespoons of bean liquid is crucial to get it smooth. Add liquid as needed to achieve the right consistency.

Chill in the refrigerator until it is time to serve. Serve with chips, peeled and sliced carrots, celery, red pepper, etc.

This is fresh, healthy, low fat, high fiber, and tasty! Of course, you can buy prepared hummus, but with canned garbanzo beans in the cupboard along with lemons and tahini in the refrigerator, you can do it yourself, on very short notice.

I recently discovered 8 cans of garbanzo beans in my cupboard. Perhaps that is overkill.

Asparagus Wrapped in Prosciutto
2-4 per person

Thinly sliced prosciutto cut in half lengthwise
Fresh asparagus, washed, peeled at the bottom, and cut to the size you want
Extra virgin olive oil
Kosher salt and coarse ground pepper, or Thyme for Salt or Tuscan Rosemary Salt (pages 54 and 55)
Parmesan cheese, finely grated

Coat the asparagus in olive oil and lightly salt and pepper. Roll the prosciutto around the asparagus so that they are almost covered but leave the top and bottom clear.

Roast in a 400° preheated oven for 10 minutes, more or less. Remove from the oven and sprinkle with finely grated Parmesan cheese, or add the cheese just before removing from the oven so it browns. Serve with a smile!

Alternative (bread in place of prosciutto):
Buy white sandwich bread, cut off the crust, and roll the bread with a rolling pin to flatten it. Spread softened cream cheese on the bread and sprinkle lightly with Parmesan cheese and salt and pepper. Roll the cheesed bread around the asparagus, place cut-side down on a baking sheet with sides, brush the bread with melted butter, and bake in a preheated 400° oven for 10 minutes, more or less.

In the past this was a spring appetizer because asparagus had a limited growing season. Fortunately for us, it is now available year round.

The fact that it is also pretty healthy should commend it as a staple for cocktail parties. You may even get requests to make it!

Meatloaf Paté
serves a party

1 pound chicken breasts, skinned, de-boned, and cut into bite-sized pieces
¼ pound bacon, cut into 1-inch pieces
¼ pound ham, cut into 1-inch pieces
1 clove of garlic, cut in half
1 shallot, cut in quarters
1 egg
1 tablespoon brandy, the good stuff if you have it
½ teaspoon coarse ground black pepper
Kosher salt, if your ham and bacon have little, about ½ teaspoon
⅛ teaspoon cinnamon
2 bay leaves

Combine the chicken and bacon with the garlic and shallot and add them to a food processor fitted with the metal blade. Process until minced. Add the ham, egg, and remaining ingredients and process until the ham is finely chopped.

Transfer the meat mixture to a loaf pan or rectangular terrine and pack it in firmly. Smooth the top and press in 2 bay leaves. Bake in a preheated 400° oven 45 minutes until the paté has pulled away from the sides and the top is nicely browned. It may take a few minutes more or less depending on your oven.

Ideally, cool and refrigerate 1 day to let the flavors develop. Slice and serve with crackers or thinly sliced bread and a good mustard.

This is a simple and not too rich version of a French country paté. It is meant to be eaten cold, and you may find it makes a great sandwich. A better version of sandwich meat! Who knew you could do it yourself?

Whitefish Spread
serves a party

1 pound smoked whitefish, skinned and deboned
3 ounces cream cheese
3 tablespoons mayonnaise
¼ cup chopped green or sweet onions
2 tablespoons capers, drained and chopped
2 tablespoons strained lemon juice (juice of 1 lemon)
1 tablespoon Worcestershire sauce
1 clove garlic, chopped fine
¼ teaspoon cayenne pepper

Starting with the cream cheese, add each of the ingredients in the order listed to a food processor, pulsing each time. Then add the whitefish, picked over to eliminate bone, skin, and any part that looks bad. Blend the mixture to create a spread. If you prefer a dip rather than a spread, add more mayonnaise to reach your desired consistency.

Serve in a small dish with crackers or crostini (toasted slices of French bread).

Crostini:
Slice a baguette ¼ inch thick. Pour extra virgin olive oil on a rimmed baking sheet. Spread the sliced baguette on the oil-covered sheet and bake at 350° for 10 minutes. Remove the crostini from the oven and turn over on the baking sheet. Sprinkle with salt and pepper. If the crostini needs a little more baking, return to the oven, perhaps with the oven off so you don't overcook.

This is a Northern Michigan specialty. Everyone who makes a whitefish spread claims theirs is the best. Make this recipe and then compare. You may soon be bragging, too.

Feel free to adjust and make it your own, even using salmon or other smoked fish. Don't forget to write it down on this page!

Avocado Tomato Salsa
serves a party

2 cloves garlic, minced or chopped fine
¼ cup Vinaigrette in a Jar (from first cookbook) or Italian dressing
2 tablespoons fresh cilantro or flat leaf parsley, chopped
½ teaspoon cumin
4 medium tomatoes, peeled, seeded, and diced
3 medium avocados, peeled, seeded, and diced (not mashed)
1 lime cut into wedges
½ cup sliced black olives
¼ cup crumbled feta cheese

Combine the minced garlic, salad dressing, cilantro, and cumin in a small bowl and set aside. Add the tomatoes to a large bowl and add the avocados as you dice them, squeezing a wedge of lime on the avocado each time. Add the olives and toss with the reserved dressing mixture. The mixture can be refrigerated briefly before the party starts.

Transfer to an appropriate serving bowl and top with the feta cheese. A few dashes of hot sauce before you add the feta will give it a little kick and you can start tasting with your favorite tortilla chips.

This appetizer is a favorite of Barb VerHage, who often brought it to our office when we celebrated a birthday. She got the original recipe from a friend and continues to give the credit. We don't believe it anymore, it's hers!

The original recipe used much more salad dressing, but it isn't needed. You decide for yourself. If you like hot sauce, you can add it as you toss the tomatoes and avocados.

What about onions? A Vidalia or sweet onion is a great option, diced and added to the dressing if you want the onion to marinate or with the tomatoes if you want more crunch. You can also make the olives and feta an option.

Mexican Salsa (with Shrimp)
serves 4–8

½ cup ketchup
Juice of 2 limes
2 tablespoons extra virgin olive oil
1 tablespoon Worcestershire sauce
1 teaspoon soy sauce
1 jalapeno chile, seeded and chopped fine
½ cup sweet onion, chopped fine
½ cup coarsely chopped green olives, either Castelvetrano or pimento-stuffed green olives
1-2 tomatoes, skinned and seeded and then chopped fine
2 tablespoons cilantro, chopped fine
2 tablespoons flat Italian parsley, chopped fine
1 teaspoon dry (or 1 tablespoon fresh) oregano
¼ teaspoon kosher salt
1 pound medium shrimp (26 per pound), optional

Combine all of the wet ingredients, then the rest. Refrigerate until ready to serve with corn chips or tacos or fish.

To make this a complete appetizer, boil the shrimp and add them just before serving with plates and forks.

Salsa is so good, how could it need all of this? Try it and you will see. It has more flavor than most and is great with a main course like fajitas or tacos, with or without the shrimp.

For a real appetizer, add the shrimp and stand back as your guests dig in. So will you!

Fresh Salsa Verde

1 pound (about 6–8 medium) tomatillos, husked and coarsely chopped
1 medium sweet onion, coarsely chopped
3–4 cloves garlic, chopped fine
2–3 jalapeno peppers, seeded and coarsely chopped
Juice of 1 lime
1 handful of fresh parsley, chopped, optional
½ to 1 teaspoon kosher salt

Put the tomatillos and onion in a food processor and process, adding the remaining ingredients as the salsa becomes smooth. Add water if it is too dry and finish with the salt to taste. Process until smooth.

Chill in the refrigerator or serve immediately. It is great either way.

I had made salsa verde roasting the ingredients. It was good but not great. When I tried this on a hot summer day, I decided the extra step of roasting was a waste of time and effort.

Of course it is good with Mexican recipes or chips, but I found it was also good with tuna and other fish for dinner as well as with chicken or pork. In other words, it is worth having on hand.

Herb Cream Cheese

8 ounces cream cheese, softened
4–6 tablespoons sour cream or plain yogurt
1 small clove of garlic, chopped fine or minced
2 tablespoons fresh chopped chives
2 tablespoons fresh chopped parsley
2 tablespoons fresh chopped basil
½ teaspoon kosher salt
¼ teaspoon coarse ground black pepper

Add the cream cheese and sour cream to a food processor. Pulse until the mixture is smooth. Add the remaining ingredients and pulse until you have a beautiful green dip or spread. Taste and adjust the seasonings, pulsing and scraping down the sides to retain the smoothness.

Refrigerate until ready to serve with celery, carrots, green or red peppers, or your favorite sliced baguette, crackers, or chips.

For a lighter and less caloric dip, substitute ricotta cheese for the cream cheese.

Particularly in the summer when fresh herbs are bountiful, this is the dip to use. Now we have access to these herbs year round so if this becomes a favorite, you do not have to wait until summer.

You can also substitute other herbs to get the flavor you prefer: thyme, rosemary, oregano, cilantro, turmeric, or cayenne pepper. You can also add a little Roquefort cheese.

Caramelized Onion Relish
you will want more

1 large sweet onion, quartered and sliced thin
2 tablespoons butter
1 tablespoon extra virgin olive oil
1 tablespoon dark brown sugar (light will do)
1 tablespoon capers, drained and chopped (optional)
½ teaspoon Thyme for Salt (page 54) or ¼ teaspoon each kosher salt and coarse ground black pepper

Heat the onion, butter, olive oil, and brown sugar in a frying pan until softened. Add the capers if you are using them along with the salt and pepper and continue to cook until they caramelize.

Serve on steaks, sandwiches, burgers, pulled pork, tacos, or salad with blue cheese.

As an appetizer:
Top crostini (page 11) with caramelized onion, thinly sliced roasted red pepper, and goat cheese. Heat in the oven for 5 minutes at 350° until the cheese softens and serve.

Or try the Mushroom and Onion Bruschetta on the next page, since you already have the onion.

You can see I am conflicted. Caramelized onion is not merely an ingredient in recipes, it is an end in itself. Then you decide how you want to use it. And you will.

I caramelize onion in my cast iron frying pan and have it cooking while I do other things. That makes it a bonus and helps me feel it was no work at all. If you should happen to make too much, save it and use it later. You will be pleased.

Mushroom and Onion Bruschetta
serves 4-8 as an appetizer, 2-4 for a main course

1 pound mushrooms, button, baby bella, and/or shiitake (without stems), sliced
2 tablespoons extra virgin olive oil
1 tablespoon butter
1 large shallot, chopped fine
1 teaspoon dried thyme
1 scant teaspoon kosher salt
½ teaspoon coarse ground black pepper
1 tablespoon white balsamic (or red wine) vinegar
¼ to ½ cup heavy cream
Parmesan cheese, grated

Saute the sliced mushrooms in the oil and butter. Once they start to caramelize, add the shallot, thyme, salt, and pepper. You can hold the mushrooms at this point, and before serving, heat them and add the vinegar and then the cream. Boil down until you like the thickness of the sauce.

For a main course:
Serve on a thick slice of sourdough bread toasted on both sides, topped first with warm caramelized onion (see previous page) and then the mushrooms and finally with grated Parmesan cheese. For appetizers, serve the same way in more modest amounts on toasted crostini (page 11). You may, of course, omit the onion and simply have Mushroom Bruschetta.

I made this first as a main course, in an effort to break up our dinner menu routine. It was an immediate hit! I had also made a salad which I bagged before adding the dressing because we ate this whole recipe. Too much of a good thing. You decide.

We were much more reserved thereafter. But it was that good. As an appetizer, it was all that was needed but Pickled Asparagus (page 18) is a great complement.

Pickled Asparagus
makes 6-8 pint jars

6-8 pint canning jars (preferably wide mouth)
4-5 pounds fresh asparagus, washed, peeled at the end, and cut a little shorter than the jars
6 cups white vinegar
6 cups water
4½ tablespoons kosher salt
1½ tablespoon sugar
1 clove garlic per jar
¼ teaspoon red pepper flakes per jar
2 tablespoons pickling spice tied into a cheesecloth bundle

Wash and sterilize jars and tops (boil for 10 minutes and leave until ready) and put ¼ teaspoon pepper flakes and 1 clove garlic in each jar. Fit the asparagus in the jars with the tips at the top. Cut any that are too long so that they fit in the jars with at least ¼ inch space at the top. 5 pounds asparagus may be too much, but use the rest for dinner, soup (from this book), or appetizer (from this book).

In a 3-quart pot, bring the vinegar, water, sugar, salt, and bundle of spices to a boil. Fill the jars with the boiling liquid to within ¼ inch of the rim of each jar. Wipe the jar rims, put on two-piece lids and fasten the screw bands. Put the jars on a rack in a deep kettle half-full of boiling water and add more water to cover the lids by an inch or two. Bring the pot to a boil for 5 minutes. Let cool and remove the jars. Let the pickled asparagus mellow a few weeks, if you can.

I find my enthusiasm for fresh asparagus in season outweighs our ability to eat it. That means we will have fresh asparagus in the refrigerator and no plans to eat it all. What to do? Pickle it! Or Asparagus Soup (page 30).

If you don't have the time to go through the processing in hot water, you will need to pickle thin asparagus because it needs the hot water to cook.

This is likely to be one of the most impressive appetizers you can produce from your cupboard/refrigerator at the last minute. It's healthy and on a hot summer day the cold asparagus will be a hit.

Bread and Butter Pickles
makes 1 quart jar

1 quart canning jar
2 seedless cucumbers
3 sprigs of fresh dill
3 cups cider vinegar
½ cup light brown sugar
1 tablespoon kosher salt
2 teaspoons coriander seeds
½ teaspoon black peppercorns
¼ teaspoon allspice berries

Wash the quart jar and top and rinse in boiling or very hot water. Place the dill in the jar. Slice the cucumbers crosswise ⅛-inch thick using a very sharp knife or mandolin. Pack the sliced cucumbers in the jar.

In a saucepan, heat the vinegar, sugar, salt, and spices, stirring until boiling and the sugar is dissolved. Pour the vinegar through a strainer into the jar. Allow to cool, place the lid on the jar, and seal.

Refrigerate and serve cold.

If it's this easy, why didn't we do it before? The answer is volume and processing. Pickle-making, like jam or preserves, require a lot of fresh ingredients, jars, and time.

This is just one jar, which you will preserve with refrigeration, not processing. You can't do this with whole dill pickles because they won't cook enough to be tender.

You might add a quarter cup of thinly sliced onion as you fill the jar for extra flavor.

Pickled Red Onions
makes 1 quart jar

1 quart canning jar
1 large red onion, thinly sliced
½ cup apple cider vinegar
1 cup warm water
1 tablespoon sugar
1½ teaspoons kosher salt

Wash the quart jar and top and rinse in boiling or very hot water. Place the onion slices in the jar. Pour the vinegar mixture over the onions and let sit at room temperature for at least 1 hour. Place the sealed jar in the refrigerator for at least 1 day, but if you can't wait, give them a try!

Refrigerate for a few weeks and serve cold on top of tacos, nachos, sandwiches, salads (especially Caesar), burgers, and whatever you can imagine.

This is so easy, why wasn't it already a staple in your refrigerator? Now it can be!

The red onion is crucial for the appearance. You could use a white onion and add food coloring, but then you'd have to answer to your health-food friends.

If you fail to keep a jar in your refrigerator, all you really need is the red onion and in 15 minutes, plus the cooling time, you are good to go.

Salads

Buttermilk Salad Dressing
many salads or a great dip

1-2 scallions (green onions), trimmed and chopped, or 1 small shallot, chopped
1 clove garlic
1 tablespoon fresh squeezed lemon juice
1 tablespoon Dijon mustard
1 tablespoon mayonnaise
1 tablespoon extra virgin olive oil
½ cup buttermilk
¼ teaspoon kosher salt
¼ teaspoon coarse ground black pepper

Combine all of the ingredients except the buttermilk in a food processor or blender and process. Add the buttermilk and process again.

Refrigerate in a container (a glass jar is perfect) until you are ready to serve.

I like ranch dressing, but I am also horrified at all of the extra ingredients in commercial dressings. This is the homemade solution! Of course, a little blue cheese on the salad will go well with this.

I also like to find uses for buttermilk left over from pancakes, blue cheese dressing, or buttermilk pie. Eureka!

Simple Caesar Salad
serves 4-8

½ loaf Italian or sourdough bread, crust cut off and cubed
2 small cloves garlic, or 1 large clove, cut in half
1 head romaine lettuce, washed, dried, and torn into pieces without the core or simply cut cross-wise with the core
1 tablespoon mayonnaise
1 teaspoon Dijon mustard
1 teaspoon Worcestershire sauce
Juice of 1 lemon, strained
Kosher salt and coarse-ground black pepper to taste
¼ cup (more or less) extra virgin olive oil
½ cup finely grated Parmesan cheese

Fry the croutons in the olive oil with half of the garlic, minced (one squeeze of a mincer), and fry until crisp and lightly browned. Set aside.

In a bowl, combine the mayo, mustard, Worcestershire, lemon, salt, and pepper and whisk. Drizzle in the olive oil until you have a creamy dressing. Taste and adjust the salt and pepper. Toss enough of the dressing with enough of the romaine lettuce to serve 4. Save the remaining lettuce and dressing for another salad or make it for 6–8. Add the croutons and toss, then add the cheese and toss again.

Serve on individual plates. Enjoy!

There are two missing ingredients as compared to the original Caesar Salad created by Caesar Cardini in his Tijuana restaurant in 1924: a coddled egg and anchovies. Oh, and he made it tableside.

Many recipes use a raw egg or an egg cooked 1 to 1.5 minutes. We keep reading about the risk of eating uncooked eggs, let alone the fussiness of that process. Really good anchovies are also hard to find. So I wanted to get close without those steps. Try it! Close enough?

Moroccan Lentil Salad
serves 6+

1 lemon, zest and juice
1 orange, juiced and strained
1 shallot, chopped fine
1 clove garlic, chopped fine
2 tablespoons honey
¼ cup extra virgin olive oil
¼ teaspoon each ginger, cinnamon, allspice, and black pepper
½ teaspoon cumin
1 teaspoon kosher salt
½ cup each raisins, grated carrots, and sliced toasted almonds
½ cup quinoa toasted, and then cooked in vegetable broth until tender, then drained
1 cup lentils, cooked in vegetable stock until tender, then drained
1 cup chickpeas, drained and rinsed

Combine all of the wet ingredients (except the olive oil) and all of the spices and whisk each to combine. Then combine the wet and dry ingredients, slowly whisking in the olive oil to create a vinaigrette.

Combine the almonds, raisins, carrots, quinoa, lentils, and chickpeas in a bowl and stir in the vinaigrette to combine. Adjust the salt and pepper and allow the salad to rest for at least 30 minutes to absorb the vinaigrette. Refrigerate, covered, until you are ready to serve.

Are you looking for a really healthy salad to make ahead? Now you have found it. That it also tastes great is just a bonus.

You can toast the almonds and quinoa in a frying pan, separately, stirring as they are heated.

What if you don't have any quinoa or chickpeas? Many beans can be substituted, great northern or black beans, either cooked in broth if they are dry beans or drained and rinsed if they are canned.

Wilted Salad
your choice!

1 slice of crisp bacon, crumbled, for every 2 people, reserving the grease in the pan
1 hard-boiled egg, chopped, for every 2 people
Boston, Bibb, or iceberg lettuce, washed, dried, and torn into small (2–3 inches) pieces
Thinly sliced sweet or red onion
Thinly sliced red pepper (optional)
Cider vinegar or white balsamic vinegar
Kosher salt and coarse ground black pepper to taste

In a salad bowl, mix the lettuce and onion (and red pepper). Have the bacon and egg ready. Heat the bacon grease in the pan and add an equal amount of vinegar to the bacon grease. Allow it to boil slightly and then pour enough into a large salad spoon for the number of people you are serving.

Toss with salt and pepper and then add the crumbled bacon and chopped egg. Toss lightly and serve.

This was a favorite weekend salad that our mother, Barbara Hoffius, sometimes fixed. Simple, casual, and oh so good. It went equally well with fried or roast chicken, pork chops, steak, hamburgers, or chili.

She used iceberg lettuce, but that was about all we knew back then. Now that there are great lettuce varieties year round, I prefer Boston or Bibb lettuce for this salad. You can decide for yourself!

Salad Nicoise
serves 2+

1 can (5 ounce) tuna in olive oil per 2 people, drained
Mixed greens, washed and dried
½ pound fingerling, red skin, or Yukon Gold baby potatoes
½ pound French green beans, steamed or boiled, firm but tender
1 hard-boiled egg, shelled and chopped
Sweet, red, or green onions sliced thin
¼ red bell pepper, seeded and sliced thin
Nicoise olives and capers to taste

Dressing: 1 tablespoon Dijon mustard, 1–2 tablespoons chopped shallots, ½ teaspoon kosher salt, ¼ teaspoon coarse ground black pepper, ⅔ cup extra virgin olive oil, and ⅓ cup red wine vinegar or white balsamic vinegar added to a 12-ounce jar with a screw-top lid. Shake and use enough to coat the salad.

Boil the potatoes and green beans in separate sauce pans as they will be done at different times. Drain in a colander and rinse the beans in cold water to stop the cooking.

In a salad bowl, add the greens and other ingredients and toss with the salad dressing. Salt and pepper to taste. If you are serving a gang you can let them help themselves to each of the ingredients separately, starting with the greens tossed in a salad bowl with the dressing. Add a little dressing to the potatoes and beans so they soak up the flavors.

The ingredients are set for two so multiply accordingly depending on how many you are serving.

You can serve this year round, but it is especially good in the summer with fresh green beans and baby potatoes from the farmers market. Cold beer or wine and a baguette will make a perfect dinner on a summer evening with friends.

In fact, it is so good you may want to replicate it year round.

French Potato Salad
serves 4 or more

1½ pounds medium potatoes, Yukon Gold or russet, the same size, peeled
2 tablespoons kosher salt
2 tablespoons shallots, green onions, or medium onions, chopped fine
1–2 tablespoons wine vinegar
2–3 tablespoons chopped fresh parsley
1 teaspoon kosher salt
½ teaspoon coarse ground pepper

Slice the potatoes ⅛ inch thick and put in a bowl of cold water to prevent yellowing. Fill a large pot halfway full of water and add the salt and potatoes. Bring to a boil and cook about 5 minutes, so the potatoes are fork tender—not soft, not hard. Drain, saving ¼ cup of the potato water, and leave the potatoes in the pot, covered, for 5 minutes.

Chop the shallots. Put the potatoes in a bowl, tossing with the shallots, vinegar, parsley, salt, and pepper. Add a little of the potato water if the potatoes appear dry. Allow the potato salad to rest, but toss as needed to bring the flavors together.

Potato salad without mayonnaise? No fat? It can be done, and it tastes great, too!

After you have made this once, it is easy to repeat and make a regular part of your routine. It can be done in 20-30 minutes. Peeling the potatoes takes the most time.

Summer Potato Salad
serves 8 or more

3 pounds new potatoes, peeled to remove spots
2 tablespoons kosher salt
1 bunch green onions, or medium onions, chopped
1 cup celery, strings removed if you prefer, chopped like onions
¾ cup mayonnaise
½ cup sour cream
1 tablespoon mustard, yellow or Dijon as you prefer
1–2 tablespoons cider vinegar
1 teaspoon kosher salt
½ teaspoon coarse ground pepper
3 hard-boiled eggs, chopped
2–3 tablespoons chopped fresh parsley

Trim the potatoes and put in a bowl of cold water to prevent yellowing. Fill a large pot halfway full of water and add the salt and potatoes. Bring to a boil and cook about 5 minutes so that the potatoes are fork tender—not soft, not hard. Drain and chop the potatoes the size you want to eat. Put them in a bowl with the onions and celery.

Mix the remaining ingredients except the eggs and parsley and add some of the dressing to the potato mixture to the consistency and richness you prefer. Refrigerate, then add or top with the chopped hard-boiled egg and parsley before serving.

Potato salad is a classic summer picnic recipe, inside or out. This is the kind of recipe that is made with only the rarest of references to a written recipe.

If you don't already have a favorite potato salad recipe, this is a great place to start. Experiment with the ratio of ingredients and dressing until you find your favorite version.

Soups

Asparagus Soup
serves 8

2 tablespoons extra virgin olive oil
1 large sweet onion, chopped
4 cloves of garlic, chopped fine or minced
1½ pounds asparagus, washed, ends peeled, and cut to 1 inch length
32 ounces chicken or vegetable broth
1 cup heavy cream
½ teaspoon coarsely ground pepper and kosher salt to taste depending on the salt in the broth

Sauté the onion and garlic in the olive oil until softened. Add the asparagus and broth and cook approximately 20–30 minutes. Blend with an immersion blender until smooth. You can stop here, adding the pepper and salt to taste and refrigerate for later. Add the cream before serving and heat but do not boil.

Like many cream soups, top with chopped fresh (or dry) parsley or chives, maybe a few croutons. Enjoy!

When asparagus is fresh in the spring, I often get enthusiastic; I want to support the farmers, and I buy way more than I have plans to serve.

My backup plan is this Asparagus Soup or Pickled Asparagus (page 18) or Asparagus Wrapped in Prosciutto (page 9). The soup freezes well for later (add the cream when reheating) or for lunch or dinner as the main course. All dinner needs is a green salad and fresh strawberries for dessert.

Black Bean Chili
serves 8

1 pound black beans, soaked for 6 hours or overnight, rinse and pick over
Extra virgin olive oil
1 large sweet onion, chopped
1 each green pepper, red pepper, hot pepper (poblano, ancho, habanero, or jalapeno), seeded and chopped
2 stalks celery, chopped
4–5 garlic cloves, finely chopped or minced
1 pound sausage (chorizo, andouille, Italian (hot or sweet), or your favorite)
2 boxes chicken broth (32 ounce each)
42 ounces diced tomatoes (1 28-ounce can and 1 14-ounce can)
3 tablespoons chili powder
2 tablespoons cumin
1 teaspoon each coriander and cinnamon
Kosher salt and coarse ground black pepper to taste

This can easily be a vegetarian chili by eliminating the sausage and substitute vegetable broth for chicken broth.

Of course, this is the basis for all kinds of chili and gumbo, so feel free to twist it your way. For instance, you could add shrimp in the last 5 minutes, top with grated cheddar cheese, sour cream, or chopped onion. Make it your own!

Sauté onion, peppers, garlic, and celery in a little extra virgin olive oil until translucent. Add sausage, either broken up or sliced thin, and continue cooking. Once the sausage is cooked, add the remaining ingredients and cook at least 1 hour.

Taste and adjust seasoning. Of course, it will taste even better the next day.

Chicken Noodle Soup
serves 8-12

64 ounces chicken broth (2 32-ounce boxes)
1 cup white wine, dry vermouth will do, (optional)
1 pound boneless, skinless chicken breast (approximately 2 large breasts), chopped
4 tablespoons butter or extra virgin olive oil
1 large onion (sweet, white, or yellow), finely chopped
2 stalks celery, finely chopped
2 carrots, peeled and finely chopped
½ pound white mushrooms, thinly sliced
¼ pound fresh green beans, trimmed and sliced diagonally into 1-inch slices
2 teaspoons kosher salt
1 teaspoon coarse ground pepper
¼ pound egg noodles, your preference, thin or wide
3 tablespoons fresh parsley, chopped

Heat the chicken broth and wine in a large saucepan to boiling and then reduce the heat and simmer with the chicken. Sauté onion, celery, carrots, and mushrooms in the butter or oil until the onions are translucent, then add the broth. Add the green beans and noodles and cook until they are cooked and ready to eat.

Taste and adjust seasoning and add fresh parsley before serving.

This is one of those recipes we seldom make from scratch anymore. Are we hooked on chicken noodle soup in a can? Or has it spoiled us from taking on such a simple soup? Like the other recipes in this book: a little planning and effort brings a great result.

Left-over chicken is a great place to start. The celery and carrots don't have to be finely chopped, thinly sliced will do just fine. How do you prefer your chicken noodle soup? Modify this recipe and make it!

Frogmore Stew
serves 8-12

2 tablespoons extra virgin olive oil
2 tablespoons Old Bay Seasoning
2 medium onions, chopped small
2 pounds link sausage (andouille, chorizo, Italian [hot or sweet] or your favorite)
2 pounds redskin or other new potato, slightly peeled to remove blemishes and cut up so they are approximately 1-inch size
1 pound frozen corn (loose, off the cob)
2 pounds peeled and deveined shrimp
1 box (28–32 ounce) seafood, chicken, or vegetable broth
1 pint Half and Half
Kosher salt and coarse ground pepper to taste

Prick the skins of the sausages, then roast them in a rimmed oven pan in a 350° oven until just cooked through. Allow the sausages to cool and then remove the skins and slice the sausage in 1-inch pieces.

Sauté onion in a pot until translucent and add the potatoes and cook until they are cooked through. Then add the Old Bay Seasoning, the sausage and broth, and stop here and save for dinner. Bring the pot to almost boiling and add the corn and finally the shrimp 10 minutes before serving, allowing the shrimp to cook through, to a beautiful pink. Add the Half and Half, and adjust the seasonings with salt and pepper.

This is a South Carolina specialty often referred to as a Lowcountry Boil. It is often cooked outside in a large pot using double these quantities and corn on the cob, cut in half or thirds. The broth is omitted and a basket is used to lift the stew out of the pot full of water. In other words, no bowl is needed. It's messy but delicious.

I've adapted the original recipe for the dining room. It is close to a one-dish meal, plus cornbread or a baguette for sopping up the broth. You can also serve over rice but that is just another dish to prepare.

Cioppino - Fish Stew
serves 8

3 tablespoons extra virgin olive oil
4 cloves garlic, peeled and chopped
1 medium white onion, peeled and chopped
2 stalks celery, sliced thin
½ large (or 1 medium) fennel bulb, quartered and sliced thin
½ green pepper, or poblano pepper, seeded and sliced thin
1 box low-sodium chicken broth (or seafood broth), 32 ounces, or 1 bottle clam juice and water to total 4 cups
1 can chopped tomatoes (28 ounces), including the juice
1 to 2 6-ounce cans crab meat
½ pound fish fillets, frozen will do but fresh is better; chopped
½ teaspoon each kosher salt and coarse ground black pepper
1 tablespoon each dry parsley and basil (or 3 tablespoons each fresh)
2 bay leaves and red pepper flakes to taste

Sauté the garlic, onion, celery, fennel, and green pepper until soft. Add broth and tomatoes and bring to a simmer for at least 30 minutes. You can add the spices and stop here until dinner or the next day. Add the crabmeat and fish, chopped, and continue simmering until the fish is cooked. Alternatively, sauté the fish separately and add it to the stew before serving.

Serve in large soup bowls with focaccia or a baguette.

You could have virtually all of these ingredients on hand with canned crabmeat and frozen fish. Fennel would be the only challenge and you can substitute other fresh ingredients, like leeks, shallots, or red pepper.

If you want to show off, use fresh crab, fish, scallops, shrimp, and/or clams, cut up as needed. However, you have added substantially to the preparation time and cost.

This is so healthy you'll feel great about making it part of your routine.

Shrimp Chowder
serves 8

1 pound shrimp (shells on will improve the broth), chopped
4 cups seafood or chicken broth (32-ounce box)
1 pound Yukon Gold or other potatoes, peeled and chopped small
1 medium yellow or white onion, peeled and chopped
2 stalks celery, strings peeled, sliced thin and chopped
1 cup white wine (dry vermouth will do)
1 teaspoon each dried parsley and thyme
½ teaspoon each kosher salt and coarse ground black pepper
1 pint heavy cream or Half and Half
2 bay leaves
Red pepper flakes to taste
Chopped green onions to garnish

Peel and devein the shrimp and put the shells in the broth and bring to a boil. Remove (strain) the shells from the broth and add half of the potatoes to the broth and simmer. Sauté the onion and celery until soft and add them to the broth, bringing it all to a simmer until the potatoes are soft. Add the wine, spices, and one-half of the shrimp and cook until the shrimp turns pink. Using an immersion blender, blend until the broth mixture is smooth.

Add the remaining potatoes and cook until almost soft. Finally, add the cream and remaining shrimp and cook until the shrimp turns pink.

Serve in bowls garnished with the chopped green onion.

Do you have to use fresh shrimp? Of course not, but the broth will be that much more flavorful. So if you're buying the shrimp and have time to peel and devein them, the results will be better. A bottle of clam juice is a good replacement for the shells or a good addition to the broth.

This is the perfect recipe for when you have shrimp left over from a party. Make this chowder the following day for a delicious lunch!

Tomato Bisque with Fresh Goat Cheese
serves 4

2 tablespoons extra virgin olive oil
2 cloves garlic, minced
1 teaspoon ginger powder or 1 tablespoon grated ginger
1 medium onion chopped fine
1 28-ounce can crushed Italian plum tomatoes
1 tablespoon sugar
1 teaspoon kosher salt
½ teaspoon red chili flakes
1 cup water
4 ounces good quality fresh goat cheese

Put olive oil in a large saucepan and heat. Add garlic and ginger and sauté until softened. Add onion and continue cooking until it too is translucent.

Add tomatoes, sugar, salt, chili flakes, and water and cook at medium for 30 minutes more or less until it looks like soup. Use an immersion blender to puree to a smooth soup. Hold at this point until ready to serve. Add cut-up pieces of goat cheese and stir, cooking until the soup is smooth, but some of the goat cheese is still visible.

Serve in bowls, perhaps with croutons, and enjoy!

It's the simplicity of it all. Tomatoes, onion, and garlic with goat cheese! The only thing you need to buy is the fresh goat cheese. Be sure it is fresh, crumbly, and ready to eat.

If you have seen fresh goat cheese in cheese shops and didn't know what to do with it, now you do!

English Pea Soup

serves 8 or more

1 large white or yellow onion, chopped fine
2 tablespoons extra virgin olive oil
48 ounces chicken broth, heated and reduced to 40 ounces
2 packages English peas, 10 ounces each, or 4 cups fresh
4 cups Bibb or Boston lettuce, washed, dried and chopped
½ teaspoon kosher salt
½ teaspoon coarse ground black pepper
½ cup heavy cream, beaten slightly to thicken but still pourable to drizzle in each bowl

Cook the onions in the olive oil until translucent. Cook the broth separately and reduce before adding it to the onion. Then add the peas and lettuce, salt and pepper, and cook about 30 minutes.

Use an immersion blender to puree the soup before serving. Add a touch of cream and croutons (see the Simple Caesar Salad recipe on page 23).

This is a perfect soup for a special lunch with a salad to complete the picture. Salad first and then the soup. What a day! Friends for life! Oh yeah, that's why you invited them.

Of course, fresh peas are even better, but it's a shame to limit this special soup to the 3 weeks when English peas are in season.

Workout Potassium Broth
serves 2 for 1 week

46 ounce V-8 tomato-based juice, low sodium
2 cups water
3 cups chopped vegetable trimmings (bell peppers, carrots, celery
    tops, lettuce, mushrooms, onion, parsley, zucchini, etc.)
1 teaspoon, or less, chili pepper flakes (optional)
1 teaspoon dry basil or thyme

Combine all of the ingredients in a soup pot and bring to a boil. Reduce heat and simmer for 1 hour covered.

Strain and press the chopped vegetables to release all of the liquid. Discard the the solids or compost. Return the broth to the V-8 bottle and add water if it isn't full.

Serve hot or cold to boost blood sugar level and replace potassium and sodium lost through perspiration. It is especially effective mid-morning before a workout later that day and after a workout.

This could be the best summer drink you have ever had. Now keep active and enjoy a hot summer!

In summer, when we have plenty of fresh vegetables, it is easy to gather the trimmings for this broth. Get in the habit, and this will become part of your routine. A 4-ounce serving may be all you need.

Vegetables

Zucchini Gratin
serves 4-6

1 large sweet onion, chopped fine
4 small zucchini (or yellow squash), approximately 1 pound, sliced ¼-inch thick
2 tablespoons extra virgin olive oil
1 tablespoon flour
1 teaspoon kosher salt
½ teaspoon coarse ground black pepper
½ cup hot milk
4 ounces Gruyere cheese, grated
¾ cup bread crumbs, cracker crumbs, or panko breadcrumbs
2 tablespoons butter

Salt zucchini and place in a colander to sweat, approximately 20 minutes. Sauté the onion in the olive oil until translucent. Add the zucchini to the onions and cook until still firm but tender. Combine the flour and salt and pepper and stir into the onion/zucchini mixture. Add the hot milk to the zucchini. Add the Gruyere cheese to the zucchini and stir it in to combine. Add the zucchini mixture to a buttered 9x9-inch baking dish.

Meanwhile, melt the butter, add the bread crumbs, and stir to combine. Top the zucchini with the breadcrumbs and bake at 350° for 30–45 minutes until bubbling.

I know you have heard the zucchini jokes about friends who found they had so many zucchini they put them on porches without a message. Any way to dispose of them.

Here is a better solution! How many nights can you eat it? Every night! Better yet, give away casseroles.

Roasted Cauliflower
serves 4–8

1 head cauliflower, stemmed, trimmed, and the flowers cut into serving-sized pieces
Extra virgin olive oil
1 clove garlic, minced
1 teaspoon dried thyme (1 tablespoon fresh)
1 teaspoon dried savory or oregano (1 tablespoon fresh)
½ teaspoon each coarse ground black pepper, kosher salt (1 teaspoon Tuscan Rosemary Salt on page 55 can replace all the spices)

Put the pieces of cauliflower in a bowl and toss with the remaining ingredients, using just enough olive oil to coat. Place the coated cauliflower in a baking dish, 9 x 12 inches. Bake in a preheated 400° oven for 20 minutes or until the cauliflower is tender. Toss and serve.

You could also sprinkle with grated fresh Parmesan, but it doesn't need it. That's just for those trying to find another excuse for freshly grated Parmesan.

Cauliflower Steak Alternative:
Slice the cauliflower in 1-inch slices and cook in a frying pan or large baking sheet with sides, coating with olive oil. Allow the first side to caramelize, flip and add the same spices as above, and caramelize the second side. Serve very happy guests!

For years I used cauliflower in roasted vegetables on the grill. It just never occurred to me that I could do them alone. The size of the cauliflower will determine how many you can serve. For a large group you may need more than one head.

You could cover this with the cream-based cheese sauce so familiar to cauliflower dishes, but you would have to skip the rest of the meal because your vegetable would have maxed out your fat and calories for the rest of the day!

Brussels Sprouts
serves 4, maybe more

1 pound Brussels sprouts, trimmed off the stalk (1 stalk of Brussels sprouts should be enough), trim off loose or colored outer leaves
Extra virgin olive oil
¼ teaspoon coarse ground pepper
½ teaspoon kosher salt, more or less to taste

Cut Brussels sprouts in half and place them cut-side down on a baking pan lightly oiled with extra virgin olive oil. Spray the tops of the sprouts with oil and bake at 375°. Bake until they are as crisp as you prefer. Toss with salt and pepper and serve.

These are great hot, but can also be served at room temperature. The problem is that if you start eating them before dinner, you may have to call them an appetizer, they are that good!

I had avoided Brussels sprouts at the market out of ignorance and poorly prepared sprouts at Thanksgiving. This recipe turned things around. It is fun to start with the sprouts on the stalk. Smaller is better and trim off the loose outer leaves.

Alternative:
Thinly slice Brussels sprouts and ½ cup shallots, sauté with a little olive oil and butter and season with Thyme for Salt (page 54) until caramelized. Wow!

Creamed Fresh Spinach
serves 2, maybe 4

1 pound spinach, fresh from the farmers market or the garden, washed, stemmed, and dried, but some water is okay so you won't have to add water to cook
2–4 tablespoons heavy cream
1–2 tablespoons prepared horseradish
Kosher salt and coarse ground black pepper to taste
1 hard-boiled egg, sliced

Put the moist spinach in a 12-inch frying pan with a little water in the bottom, 1 tablespoon should do it. Heat the spinach, covered, over medium heat until it wilts into the bottom of the pot. Stir and add the cream, horseradish, salt and pepper. It really does not take much cream or horseradish. Start with the lesser amounts indicated before jumping to the maximum, you too may be surprised how little is enough.

Serve immediately in two small dishes (if you want to avoid the cream running all over the plate) with half a sliced egg over each serving.

This is a favorite both because of the care that is needed to wash and stem the spinach, and because of the "less is more" design of the recipe.

You will find Creamed Spinach recipes with onions, garlic, nutmeg, and Parmesan cheese. I know they are good, but if you have access to really fresh spinach, why cover up its essence? In other words, this is a very special summer treat!

Could you make a pound serve four? Of course! In fact, you will just be highlighting how special it is by serving each person less.

Swiss Chard
serves 2

½ medium-sized Vidalia or sweet onion, thinly sliced
1 tablespoon extra virgin olive oil
½ pound (plus) Swiss chard, washed, stemmed, dried, and torn into pieces
Kosher salt and coarse ground black pepper to taste
Splash or 2 of cider vinegar

Put the olive oil in a large pan (with a cover which you will need for the Swiss chard) and add the onions. Sauté the onions about 15 minutes over low-to-medium heat. Salt and pepper the onions.

Add the Swiss chard and cover. The Swiss chard will wilt in 2–3 minutes. Toss the Swiss chard with a fork so that the onions are mixed in. Splash on the cider vinegar. It is a seasoning, not an ingredient, so less is more. Serve and enjoy.

Obviously, this recipe can be adjusted depending on the size of the gathering. However, based on the time to prepare the Swiss chard, it is a wonderful dish for two!

Our farmers market has absolutely beautiful Swiss chard, and I had to figure out how to fix it. After looking at way too many recipes, I came up with this. It is simple and flavorful.

I start the onions while I am working on the rest of the dinner and hold the onions if they caramelize too soon. I tried more cider vinegar at first and concluded it needed only a little to season, not to flood, the Swiss chard.

Snow Peas
serves 4

32 snow peas (about 8 peas per person)
Water, just covering the bottom of a small pan
Blue cheese, about two tablespoons or two small slices

Wash and stem the snow peas down both sides. Put the peas in a pan (with a cover which you will need when you add the cheese) and add water to just cover the bottom. Heat on medium until the water is about to evaporate from the pan, about three minutes. Add the blue cheese and cover. You may just turn off the heat and tend to other business.

Serve 8 peas per person along with the melted blue cheese, awarding the guest of honor (or the server) the extra cheese at the bottom.

Sesame Alternative:
Use the same amount of peas, but once they are cooked and the water has just disappeared, simply toss in toasted or dark sesame oil, toasted sesame seeds, and kosher salt or Thyme for Salt (recipe on page 54).

This was a friend's specialty, but she was reluctant to tell the secret to its success. I think this is close.

Once you get it, you will be making it regularly!

The sesame alternative is a nice way to break up your routine.

Roasted Fennel (3 Ways)
serves 4-6

4 medium fennel, cut in half and sliced thin
4 medium sweet onions or 1 large, cut in half or quarters and sliced thin
Extra virgin olive oil
Approximately 1 teaspoon Thyme for Salt (page 54)
Heavy cream
Parmesan cheese (optional)

1. Toss the fennel and onion in olive oil and season with salt and pepper. Roast in a 400° oven for approximately 1 hour, tossing once or twice.

2. Same as 1 but use only cream and no or barely any olive oil.

3. Eliminate the onion and use either the oil or cream, increasing the fennel so that there is 1 per person.

Serve hot out of the oven. Top with grated Parmesan cheese, or not.

This recipe is easily prepared and needs little attention. In fact, the timing of tossing creates a special roasted effect.

It's included in the Vegetables section, but I have used it in place of a potato with a vegetable. If healthier is your goal, stick with the olive oil and go light.

Side Dishes

Twice-Baked Potato Casserole
serves 8

3–6 russet potatoes, about 2 pounds, washed, scrubbed, and pierced with a fork
¾ cup shallots (1 small/medium shallot per potato), chopped very fine or grated
2 tablespoons butter
½ pound extra-sharp cheddar cheese, grated
2 teaspoons kosher salt, less if you use fewer potatoes
1 teaspoon coarse ground black pepper
1½ cups sour cream

Bake the potatoes in a preheated 400° oven until tender, about 1 hour. Cool, preferably overnight in a plastic bag in the refrigerator.

Preheat the oven to 350°. Sauté the shallots in the butter until they are translucent. Grate the potatoes using a box grater with the large holes. You do not need to skin the potatoes but do cut out any parts of the skin you do not want to end up in the casserole. Throw out any skin that does not get grated. Place the grated potatoes in a bowl and mix in the shallots and almost all of the cheese, reserving enough to top the casserole before baking. Add the salt and pepper and fold in the sour cream.

Put the potato mixture in a buttered 9 x 13 inch baking dish. Top with the remaining cheese and bake for about 30 minutes, 40 minutes if you stored it in the refrigerator.

Twice-baked potatoes are terrific for dinner but a lot of work for a party, especially when you are not sure how many will show up. This is the solution!

Of course, it is also perfect for a buffet or a pot luck. You should be so lucky to have any left over for the next night. I sometimes make it in small casseroles and use one for our dinner and hold the rest in the refrigerator or freezer for future use.

Hasselback Potato Gratin
serves 8

7–8 russet potatoes, about 4 pounds, washed, scrubbed, peeled, and sliced by hand or on a mandolin slicer ⅛-inch thick
4 ounces extra-sharp cheddar or Gruyère, grated
2 ounces Parmesan cheese, grated fine
2 cups heavy cream
2 cloves garlic, chopped fine
1 tablespoon fresh thyme leaves, chopped, or 1 teaspoon dried
2 teaspoons kosher salt, less if you use fewer potatoes
1 teaspoon coarse ground black pepper
2 tablespoons butter

Preheat oven to 400°. Combine the cheeses in a large bowl and reserve ⅓ in a smaller bowl. As topping for the potatoes, add cream, garlic, and spices to the cheeses in the large bowl and stir to combine.

Add the potato slices to the large bowl of cheese and cream and thoroughly coat potato slices. You may find that your hands are the ultimate implements for coating.

Grease a 9 x 13 inch casserole or pan with butter. Stack potato slices vertically along one edge and continue to create adjacent rows until casserole is full. Pour any excess cream over potatoes.

Cover the casserole with aluminum foil and bake 30 minutes. Remove the foil and top with the cheeses you set aside. Return the casserole to the oven for another 30 minutes or until the potatoes and cheese are a crusty brown.

This is really just a slightly better presentation of scalloped potatoes. See Just Good Food *page 67. The real challenge here is to get the right amount of potatoes to fill your casserole. The best way is to have a few extra potatoes as well as cream and cheese, just in case.*

If you have too much of a good thing, a second small casserole will fit the bill. Bake it or freeze it for another meal.

Tuscan White Beans
serves 8 or more

1 pound dry Great Northern beans
1 large box (32 or 40 ounces) chicken or vegetable broth
4 cloves garlic, chopped
1 large sweet onion, chopped
1 red pepper, seeded and chopped
1 green pepper, a hot variety or not, chopped
2 tablespoons (or more) extra virgin olive oil
1 teaspoon kosher salt
½ teaspoon coarse ground black pepper
1 tablespoon each thyme and parsley

Soak the beans overnight in a large bowl with water covering the beans. You may need to add more water as they absorb the water.

Drain the beans and add them to the broth and cook approximately 1 hour until the beans are tender. Sauté the garlic, onion, and peppers in that order until soft and add them to the tender beans and broth. Continue to cook to reduce the broth, if necessary, and add the spices. Be careful: If the broth is salty, you may not need all the salt.

If there is still too much liquid (more likely with the 40-ounce box of broth), you can drain it and cook it down in a separate pot. Garnish with fresh parsley.

This is not just a side dish! You can also serve it with toast as an appetizer, process and serve it like hummus, add one pound peeled and deveined fresh shrimp and cook five more minutes for a main dish, add chopped tomatoes (one 14-ounce can), or start it all with about ½ pound of Italian sausage and serve it as a main dish.

Roasted Sweet Potato Fries

serves 4-6

2 pounds sweet potatoes, peeled, sliced, and cut into ¼-inch rectangular strips
Extra virgin olive oil to coat the potatoes
Rattlesnake Salt (page 55) or use a mixture of 1 tablespoon kosher salt, 1 teaspoon pepper, and ½ teaspoon fennel seed ground in a mortar and pestle

Heat the oven to 425° and place the potatoes on an oiled baking sheet with sides. Toss the potatoes with the oil and add the seasonings.

Put the potatoes in the oven and cook for 20–30 minutes until they look crisp and ready to eat, tossing them as needed to even out the cooking. Add more salt if they need it. Enjoy!

We know sweet potatoes are healthier than potatoes but we need more recipes to make the transition. Here is a good place to start, and you can sell them to the kids as fries.

Sometimes at the farmers market in the fall we see those beautiful sweet potatoes, but we think of them only as a Thanksgiving dish. Forget that!

Hoppin' John
serves 4

8 ounces sausage, casings removed, chopped
1 clove garlic, minced
1 large sweet onion, chopped
12 ounce can black-eyed peas, drained and rinsed
½ cup rice, basmati or brown
1 box (32 ounces) chicken broth
1 teaspoon Tuscan Rosemary Salt, or ¼ teaspoon each kosher salt, coarse ground black pepper, thyme, and rosemary

Sauté the sausage, garlic, and onion until the sausage is starting to brown and the onion is translucent. Add the black-eyed peas and the broth and bring to a boil. Reduce the heat to a simmer and cook until the peas are tender. It won't take long with fresh or canned peas.

Add the rice and seasonings and continue simmering until the rice is cooked and the flavors incorporated. You can stop the cooking and hold until the Hoppin' John is to be (reheated and) served.

Hoppin' John is a New Year's Day specialty in the South. Eating it on January 1st will bring good luck for the year. We spent a New Year's vacation in Charleston not long after my brother Steve had moved there. Of course, we wanted to honor tradition but my attempts at Hoppin' John were not as successful as my Red Beans and Rice. It is easier to overcook Hoppin' John than Red Beans and Rice but I think I finally got it and the good luck seemed to come!

Salts & Sauces

Thyme for Salt

The ingredients in parentheses are for a larger batch in case you are supplying the neighborhood

¼ cup coarse kosher salt (1 cup)
3 tablespoons coarse ground black pepper (¾ cup)
2 tablespoons coarse ground white pepper (½ cup)
1 tablespoon thyme (¼ cup)
1 tablespoon garlic powder (¼ cup)
1 tablespoon onion powder (¼ cup)
1 teaspoon dried lemon peel (1 tablespoon & 1 teaspoon)

Use as you would salt and pepper in almost any situation (except where garlic and onion would not be appropriate). There is slightly more pepper than salt.

If you use it as if it were pepper, the salt is going along for the ride. Surprisingly, it is just about the right amount of both. None of the other flavors dominate. You may not even notice them.

I kept finding I needed a salt and pepper mixture that could be used most of the time. I started trying different combinations and finally found this to be the best.

I made a big batch and passed it out to about 20 friends. They all incorporated it in their cooking and said, "Don't mess with it!"

To buy jars of this, see the Introduction.

Rattlesnake Salt

The ingredients in parentheses are for a larger batch because your friends may beg for their own bottle.

¼ cup coarse kosher salt (1 cup)
3 tablespoons coarse ground black pepper (¾ cup)
2 tablespoons paprika (½ cup)
1 tablespoon ground white pepper (¼ cup)
1 tablespoon dried lemon peel (¼ cup)
1½ teaspoon ground cumin (2 tablespoons)
1 teaspoon garlic powder (1 tablespoon & 1 teaspoon)

Use as a seasoning for beef, pork, salmon, chicken, vegetables, potatoes, and pasta.

Tuscan Rosemary Salt

¼ cup coarse kosher salt
¼ cup crushed rosemary
2 tablespoons dried oregano
2 tablespoons garlic powder
2 tablespoons coarse ground black pepper
1 tablespoon dried crushed sage
1 tablespoon dried lemon peel

Use as a rub or seasoning for pork, veal, chicken, or fish.

Mix 2 tablespoons with 1 pound of unseasoned pork sausage to create a great sausage for pasta dishes, or sausage gravy (page 105).

These are two basic seasonings that were included in my first cookbook. I refer to them here because they are used in many of my recipes.

Rattlesnake Salt is a great gift and many who bought my first cookbook have reported to me that they have made it as a holiday or special occasion gift.

I had been making it long before the book, and friends were surprised and distressed I included the recipe. They knew they should now make it themselves.

The Tuscan Rosemary Salt is wonderful with chicken and fish as well as vegetables. Both recipes are low on salt!

To buy jars of either of these, see the Introduction.

Marinades for Flank Steak
marinates 1 steak

Number 1
¼ cup red wine vinegar
¼ cup soy sauce
¼ teaspoon each coarse ground black pepper and dried thyme
⅛ teaspoon each garlic pepper and hot sauce

Number 2
½ cup soy sauce
¼ cup red wine vinegar
1 head garlic sliced or chopped

Number 3
Juice of 1 lime
2 tablespoons soy sauce
1 teaspoon light brown sugar
½ teaspoon each ground ginger, garlic powder, coarse ground pepper, and kosher salt

Combine all ingredients and marinate the steak, covered in the refrigerator, for up to 24 hours. Drain and reserve the marinade to baste the steak on the grill. Grill and slice on the diagonal.

Of course you can use this on other steaks that need a little tenderizing.

Feel free to add ¼ cup extra virgin olive oil to help with the grilling.

These marinades will also work on pork, chops, or tenderloin, but try them first on steak.

Ravigole Sauce
serve with steak or beef

⅔ cup finely chopped onion
3 tablespoons Dijon mustard
4 tablespoons white or red wine vinegar
⅔ cup extra virgin olive oil
¼ cup capers, drained and chopped
¼ cup fresh (2 tablespoons dried) parsley
2 tablespoons shallots, minced
2 tablespoons chives or green onion, chopped
½ teaspoon dried tarragon
½ teaspoon kosher salt
¼ teaspoon coarse ground black pepper

Soak the chopped onion in cold water for 3 minutes, drain, and squeeze the onion dry in paper towels.

In a separate bowl, whisk together the mustard and vinegar. Add the oil in a steady stream, whisking until well blended. Stir in the remaining ingredients and refrigerate until dinner, removing as dinner preparations begin so that it is room temperature as it is served.

The vinaigrette (mustard, vinegar, and olive oil) can be made a day ahead and refrigerated, with the remaining ingredients added before serving.

This is a classic French sauce to serve at room temperature. It is particularly good with flank steak to provide a boost and make it very special. The sauce can be made ahead and will thereby be ready without affecting dinner preparations.

The challenge is to take it out of the refrigerator as you begin the final preparations for dinner.

If the vinaigrette is made ahead, the rest of the recipe is a perfect assignment for a dinner guest wanting to help.

Fresh Worcestershire Sauce
serves a picnic

1 teaspoon extra virgin olive oil
3 shallots, finely chopped
1 can (14.5 ounces) tomato sauce
2 cups red wine vinegar
2 tablespoons fish sauce (often labeled *nam pla* or *nuoc mam* in the Asian section)
1 teaspoon ground black pepper
1 teaspoon cardamom
1 teaspoon ground ginger
½ teaspoon cinnamon
½ teaspoon ground cloves
½ teaspoon chili powder
¼ cup honey

Heat oil in a sauce pan and sauté shallots until they caramelize. Add tomato sauce and heat, simmer 5 minutes. Remove the pan from the heat and add the all the remaining ingredients except the honey. Once the sauce is cool, add the honey and combine.

Transfer the sauce to a blender and puree until smooth. Refrigerate in clean, covered jars.

This is so good, watch who you share it with. They may beg for their own jar. Just give them the recipe.

It is easy to make, and you probably have all the ingredients, except the fish sauce. Amazingly, I had that the first time I made it. Otherwise, I might have set it aside to do later, and you know what happens then, it sits in file, perhaps forever.

Comeback Sauce
serves just enough

1 cup mayonnaise
⅔ cup bottled chili sauce (like Heinz or your favorite)
½ cup extra virgin olive oil
⅓ cup ketchup
2 tablespoons lemon juice
1 tablespoon Dijon mustard
1 tablespoon horseradish sauce
1 tablespoon Worcestershire sauce
3–5 dashes hot sauce (Frank's, Tabasco, or your favorite)
1 teaspoon each coarse ground black pepper, dried celery, garlic, ginger, kosher salt, and onion
¼ cup water

Add the wet ingredients (except the water) to a blender or food processor and blend. Then combine the dry ingredients with the water and mix before adding them to the blender. Blend all of the ingredients until a beautiful pink mixture results. Pour into a jar and refrigerate, hopefully overnight so that the flavors blend, unless you can't wait. Then a little refrigeration is better than none.

Serve with shrimp, fish, hamburgers, sandwiches, salad in place of Thousand Island dressing, or anywhere a sauce with a little kick makes it better.

This is a southern concoction with Greek roots. It is found in Mississippi and Louisiana and every recipe is a secret. This is my version; don't tell.

What can you do to create a fast version for immediate consumption?

Combine ¾ cup mayonnaise, ¼ cup sour cream or Greek yogurt, ¼ cup chili sauce or ketchup, 2 tablespoons Dijon mustard, 1 tablespoon horseradish and ½ teaspoon hot sauce. To make it your own, look at the ingredients in the full recipe and adjust a little at a time. Garlic and onion seem obvious, maybe a little lemon juice?

Whole Grain Mustard
for lots of burgers, hotdogs, and sandwiches!

¼ cup brown mustard seeds
¼ cup yellow mustard seeds
½ cup white wine (dry vermouth will do)
½ cup cold water
1 teaspoon kosher salt

Place the mustard seeds, wine, and water in a glass jar with a lid. Cover and let stand overnight. Add the salt and puree the mustard-seed mixture to the level of consistency you want. Return to the jar and cover. Store in the refrigerator for at least 24 hours before using.

Options: Add herbs, balsamic vinegar (white or dark), pepper, garlic, honey, or chopped shallot. You may want to test a little before going all the way. I would suggest honey, an herb like dry thyme, and vinegar. The objective is to season the mustard, not to overwhelm it!

I just loved being able to do this. The fact that it was easy was a factor, but not the whole story. It is also good and fun to do.

Mustard Sauce
serves 2 parties!

1 cup mayonnaise
⅓ cup Dijon mustard
¼ cup prepared horseradish, drained
¼ cup onion, finely chopped
1 teaspoon Worcestershire sauce (or less to taste)
Dash of your favorite hot pepper sauce

Mix the mayonnaise, mustard, and horseradish. Then add the remaining ingredients, stirring to combine.

Chill several hours before serving with fish, pork, chicken, beef, or on sandwiches. Of course it can also be a dip with fresh vegetables.

If you want to reduce the fat, you can substitute Greek yogurt or sour cream for some of the mayonnaise.

A sauce to build your repertoire. Again, it's all things you are likely to have on hand.

Reduce the Dijon to make it more of a horseradish sauce for beef.

How about a minced clove of garlic? Improvise!

Cranberry Ketchup
enough for Thanksgiving dinner

12 ounces (¾ pound) fresh cranberries
1 cup orange (or apple) juice
½ cup red wine vinegar
1 cup light brown sugar
1 tablespoon powdered sugar
1 teaspoon ground cinnamon
Dash of kosher salt

Wash and pick over the cranberries. Combine the cranberries with the remaining ingredients and heat in a pot over medium heat until the cranberries pop, approximately 25–30 minutes.

Cool and either serve in this popped condition, stirring to smooth out the rough edges, or process into ketchup with an immersion blender or in a food processor. Add a little water if you prefer a thinner sauce.

Okay, I see cranberry ketchup, but where's the turkey recipe? Check out the Butterflied Chicken recipe and just substitute turkey.

Beef, Pork, & Lamb

Beef Bourguignon
serves 8

2 pounds beef stew meat, cut up into 1-inch cubes
2 tablespoons extra virgin olive oil
1 large onion, chopped fine
4–6 cloves garlic, chopped fine
14-ounce can of chopped tomatoes
1 large carrot, chopped fine
32-ounce box of beef broth
2 cups red wine - Cabernet, Malbec, Merlot, Chianti, Bordeaux, etc.
1 tablespoon dried thyme and 3 bay leaves
¼ cup flour
1 teaspoon kosher salt
½ teaspoon coarse ground black pepper
Your choice of at least 3 of the following: 1 pound baby potatoes, peeled and quartered, 1 pound baby onions peeled, 1 pound mushrooms wiped and cut to a size like the onions, 1 bunch of baby carrots peeled and cut into 2-inch pieces

Sauté the chopped onion and garlic until soft. Add the stew meat and cook until it is no longer rare. Add the tomatoes, carrot, broth, wine, and spices. Cover and cook at a simmer on the stove or in the oven (325°) for 2½ hours.

Add the remaining ingredients, including the flour and the spices and stir. The recipe can be held at this point in the refrigerator until dinner. Then bring to room temperature and cook another 30 minutes until tender. Serve with a splash of fresh parsley on each serving or on the beef bourguignon if you are serving buffet style.

Let's say you've invited friends for dinner on a cold evening. What to prepare that lets you join the party and still serve a special dinner? Try this recipe!

This isn't Julia Childs, but it is inspired by her. You don't want to spend the entire day cooking, only to fall asleep at the table with the first glass of wine!

Beef Stroganoff
serves 6

2 pounds sirloin steak, trimmed and sliced thin
2 tablespoons extra virgin olive oil
2 garlic cloves, chopped fine
1 onion, chopped
1 pound mushrooms, cleaned and sliced
1–2 cans Campbell's Beef Consomme
¼ cup flour
1 tablespoon dried dill (¼ cup fresh dill, chopped)
2 cups sour cream, reserving ¼ cup for garnish
¼ cup dry white wine, dry vermouth will do
12 ounces wide egg noodles
1 tablespoon ketchup, 1 teaspoon kosher salt, ½ teaspoon coarse ground black pepper, fresh parsley

Brown the steak in olive oil, then remove to a bowl. Sauté onion, garlic, and mushrooms until soft and tender. Add the wine and the steak and deglaze the pan. Add ketchup, salt, pepper, and consomme and heat. Mix the flour in some of the liquid to create a roux and add to the mixture. Add the dill to the mixture, stirring, and heat until ready to add the sour cream. May be held at this point until you're ready to cook the noodles and add the sour cream.

Serve the stroganoff over, alongside, or mixed into the noodles. Use the extra sour cream as a topping along with fresh parsley.

This was an old favorite that was frequently served when I was growing up. I had set it aside and then made it for a gathering where I wanted to have dinner ready without much preparation after the guests arrived. Everyone made the same comment: an old favorite. Why had we set it aside?

It's beef stew with noodles, embellished with sour cream. What's not to like?

Peppered Steak in Beer & Garlic
serves 4

4 6-ounce steaks, or 2 strip steaks, or 1 sirloin up to 2 pounds
2 garlic cloves, minced
½ bottle brown ale or stout (figure out what to do with the rest)
2 tablespoons dark brown sugar (light brown will do)
2 tablespoons Worcestershire sauce
1 tablespoon extra virgin olive oil
1 tablespoon crushed black peppercorns and coarse kosher salt

Put the steak in a plastic bag and add all but the salt and pepper. Mix the marinade with the steaks in the bag so it is all well combined. Refrigerate the steaks at least 2–3 hours or overnight, turning several times. Remove the steaks and preserve the marinade to baste the steaks. Press on the salt and pepper.

Grill on medium-high heat to sear the first side, about 3–4 minutes. Baste, turn, and reduce the heat to low to medium and baste again. Cook until medium rare (130°) or medium (150°). Top with butter or a little crumbled blue cheese and allow to rest 5 minutes.

It's summer and you need an excuse to heat up the grill and relax. Roast some vegetables in a grill pan, starting a little before the steak. Include some fingerling potatoes and you have a meal and a happy family and friends. Enjoy!

Short Ribs and Swiss Chard
serves 6-8

2–3 pounds beef short ribs
4 tablespoons Rib Rub (page 69)
Kosher salt and coarse ground pepper
Flour to dust the ribs
¼ cup plus extra virgin olive oil
1 large white or yellow onion, chopped coarsely
2 stalks celery, strings peeled, and chopped
4 carrots, peeled and coarsely chopped
4 large cloves garlic, peeled
2 tablespoons dry thyme
4 cups (32-ounce box) beef broth
1 large bunch Swiss chard leaves, coarsely chopped

Combine the salt, pepper, and flour and dust the ribs. Put the olive oil in a Dutch oven and heat the ribs on all sides until browned. Remove from the pan and add the onion, celery, carrots, and garlic and saute for 3 minutes. Add the thyme and broth and heat until boiling.

Add the ribs, cover, and bake in a 350° oven for 2½–3 hours until the meat is tender and falling off the bone. Remove the ribs and set aside. Remove some of the broth and use it to create a roux by mixing flour into the broth to thicken it. Add the roux back to the pan and stir into the broth. Remove the fat from the pan. Blend the sauce in the pan using an immersion blender. Put the ribs back in the pan and return to the oven until ready to serve.

Blanch the Swiss chard in a little salted boiling water and drain. Serve the ribs over the Swiss chard. Pour the sauce over the ribs.

I have always been reluctant to fix short ribs as I focus on all of the fat. The fact is, most of the fat cooks off; you can spoon it off or just cook it down. Plus, the Swiss chard makes it seem like health food. It really doesn't need the Swiss chard but it's a real bonus.

Some people strain the sauce and don't blend it. Why lose all the good stuff?

Beef or Pork Stir Fry
serves 4

1 pound beef (flank or other steak), cut into thin strips, fat and grizzle removed, or pork (chop, tenderloin, etc.)
2 tablespoons canola oil, perhaps more with the vegetables
1 large sweet onion, sliced into 2-inch pieces
4 garlic cloves, finely chopped
1 red pepper, sliced into 2-inch slices
1 small hot pepper, chopped
1 pound (before cleaning) each of two vegetables: broccoli, green beans, cauliflower, carrots, mushrooms, tomatoes, yellow squash, or zucchini; washed, seeded, stemmed, and sliced
1 tablespoon each: soy sauce, rice vinegar, sherry or sherry vinegar, and cornstarch; and 1 teaspoon each sugar and oil (sesame or canola)
⅓ to ½-cup chicken broth, maybe more
Kosher salt and coarse ground pepper to taste

Heat a wok or large frying pan (not a non-stick pan) on high heat. Add the oil and after 15 seconds add the meat, stir, and cook about 2 minutes. Remove the meat to a plate or bowl and set aside. Add the garlic, onions, and pepper, cooking until just soft. Then add the vegetables and stir fry for several minutes.

Meanwhile, mix the soy sauce, vinegar, cornstarch, sugar, oil, and finally the broth. Add the mixture to the stir fry and cover until the vegetables steam and become tender. Add the meat, uncover, and stir, tasting for salt and pepper.

A stir fry is more of a technique than a recipe. It is an opportunity to use what you have. We often use leftover pork, beef, chicken, or salmon. Shrimp is terrific too and like cooked meat does not need to be cooked before, as it only takes 5 minutes and cooks well in the broth.

I know the broth is less than the smallest can, so freeze the rest for future use.

Two vegetables and mushrooms are a good way to get more fresh ingredients without overdoing it. Too many vegetables can result in a confusing blend of flavors. Keep it simple! Use fresh grated ginger, Worcestershire sauce, and/or ketchup for extra flavor, about a tablespoon each to start.

Savory Grilling Rub
a lot of ribs

¼ cup each: kosher salt, coarse ground black pepper, coarse ground white pepper, chili powder, sweet paprika, and dark brown sugar packed
1 tablespoon each: dry onion, garlic, basil, cumin, thyme, and oregano
1 teaspoon each: dry lemon peel, cinnamon, ginger, ground cloves, instant coffee (one Starbucks VIA package is perfect), and cocoa

Mix all of the ingredients in three steps, first the ¼ cup ingredients, then the tablespoon ingredients, and finally the teaspoon ingredients. Rub over a rack of ribs, steak, or chicken and cook in accordance with your favorite recipe.

Barbecue Sauce
all of your ribs and more

1 can (28 ounces) tomato puree
2 cups cider vinegar
1 cup honey
¼ cup Savory Grilling Rub (see above)

Combine the ingredients in the order listed and blend in a 3-quart sauce pan. Heat over medium heat until it simmers and cook at least 1 hour. Use on ribs or anywhere barbecue sauce is perfect (for instance, sautéed onions and barbecue sauce on a hamburger).

This Savory Grilling Rub works well on steak, pork, or chicken. Try it, it may be your new favorite. Only the black pepper and the chili powder are hot, and that depends on your favorite chili powder. The brown sugar caramelizes nicely on a steak.

To buy jars of this, see the Introduction.

The Barbecue Sauce is my response to all of the barbecue sauces that are loaded with fructose corn syrup. If you don't like so much vinegar, cut it back to 1 cup. If you think this is too sweet, use less honey; if you like it sweeter, use more; and if you like more spice, add 2 additional tablespoons. Make it your own!

Pork Chops in Lemon Caper Sauce
serves 4

4 bone-in pork chops, about 8 ounces each
1 teaspoon each kosher salt and coarse ground black pepper
½ teaspoon dried thyme
2 tablespoons extra virgin olive oil
2 tablespoons butter
2 garlic cloves, minced
1 small shallot, chopped fine
2 tablespoons flour
1 cup dry white wine (dry vermouth will do)
12 ounces chicken broth
2 tablespoons drained capers, 2 tablespoons lemon juice and 1 teaspoon lemon zest, and fresh or dried parsley for garnish

Season the chops with the salt, pepper, and thyme. Sauté in olive oil to brown the chops, about 5 minutes per side. Set the chops aside on a plate. Add the butter and sauté the garlic and shallots until soft. Sprinkle the flour into the pan and stir. Whisk in the wine and chicken broth and continue cooking and whisking until the sauce is reduced by half.

Stir in the capers, lemon juice, and zest and continue stirring. Add the chops to the sauce and allow them to warm. Serve 1 chop per person with sauce topping them off and finish with parsley.

Lemon caper sauce is so good on veal or chicken piccata, can it be used on other things? Yes! It is also great with fish and pork chops.

You can also use larger chops if you have a pan that will accommodate more than one. Consider serving the larger chop sliced on a platter.

Pork Medallions in Mushroom Wine Sauce
serves 4

1 pound (more or less) pork tenderloin, fat and sinews removed
Kosher salt and coarse ground black pepper
½ cup unbleached all-purpose white flour
2 tablespoons extra virgin olive oil
1 tablespoon butter
1 large shallot, chopped fine (about ¼ cup)
1 pound mushrooms, button or your favorite, sliced thin
1 can (10–12 ounce) beef broth
⅓ cup Marsala wine (or Cabernet Sauvignon, Zinfandel, etc.)
¼ cup heavy cream
2 tablespoons flat-leaf parsley, chopped (optional)

Cut the pork tenderloin into ¾-inch disks and lightly sprinkle on both sides with salt and pepper. Dredge the pork in the flour and shake off the excess. Heat the oil and butter in a heavy frying pan over medium heat. Add the floured pork and cook on one side until it browns and turn it to the other side and brown. Remove the pork to a plate and lightly cover with foil.

Sauté the chopped shallots in the pan until they are translucent (add more olive oil if needed), then add the mushrooms and cook until softened. Stirring, add the wine, the leftover flour, and the broth, and cook until the sauce thickens. Whisk in the cream and bring to a boil. Serve over the pork medallions and sprinkle with parsley.

A friend found this recipe and passed it on to me. She served it over rice. I served it over flat egg noodles, about ½ pound, but it really can be served as it is with a vegetable or potato.

The original recipe used dried mushrooms (1 ounce), rehydrating them as directed on the package. The liquid can be strained and used in place of the broth. If cleaning mushrooms is not your favorite chore, you may prefer the dried mushroom alternative.

Pork Tacos
serves 4

1 pork tenderloin, approximately 1–2 pounds, fat and sinews removed, cut into bite-size pieces
Extra virgin olive oil
Savory Grilling Rub (page 69)
Salsa, your favorite
Avocado, peeled and diced
Fresh cilantro or flat-leaf parsley, chopped
Flour tortillas, approximately 2 per person

Toss the pork pieces with olive oil to moisten and then add enough Savory Grilling Rub to season it all well. Sauté the pork in a frying pan over medium-high heat, approximately 5 minutes. Heat each tortilla on a griddle or cast-iron frying pan, turning until they start to puff. Stack them on a cloth napkin or towel, folding so that each tortilla can steam with cloth on both sides.

Assemble the tacos with pork, salsa, and avocados and sprinkle with cilantro or flat-leaf parsley. Of course, you can add chopped onions, grated cheese, hot sauce, etc. Tacos are a great buffet item with everyone embellishing their tacos their own way.

Ground beef alternative:
Sauté one medium onion, one chopped and seeded jalapeno pepper, and one chopped garlic clove with 1 pound of ground beef. Add 1 tablespoon Savory Grilling Rub (page 69) or 1 teaspoon each cumin and oregano with ½ teaspoon each kosher salt and coarse ground pepper along with ½ cup water. Cook down until ready to add to the tacos.

A simple alternative to the avocado and salsa is the Avocado Tomato Salsa (page 12). This is a great appetizer with crisp tortilla chips replacing the flour tortillas. There won"t be any left!

Rack of Lamb
serves 4

1 rack of lamb
1 cup fresh breadcrumbs
1 tablespoon chopped fresh rosemary, thyme, and flat leaf parsley
1 teaspoon kosher salt
½ teaspoon coarse black pepper
3 tablespoons extra virgin olive oil
2 tablespoons Dijon mustard

Marinade
⅓ cup dry vermouth
2 tablespoons extra virgin olive oil
2 cloves garlic and 1 shallot, chopped fine
1 teaspoon each rosemary and thyme

Prepare the marinade and add the marinade and rack of lamb in a fresh plastic bag and hold at room temperature for 1 hour.

Bring a cast-iron frying pan or stainless-steel pan to medium-high heat on the stove. Add the oil and sear the rack of lamb for 4 minutes. Combine the breadcrumbs and spices. Salt and pepper the rack, cover it with the mustard and them coat the mustard rack with the spiced breadcrumbs.

Roast the rack covered with the breadcrumbs in a preheated 400° oven to an internal temperature of 130°, approximately 20–25 minutes. Remove from the oven to a cutting board or platter and allow it to rest 10 minutes so the juices can redistribute. Slice between the bones and serve immediately.

If you refrigerate the rack before cooking, remove from the refrigerator for 1 hour to come to room temperature before cooking.

The result should be a medium-rare rack. Some servings may vary slightly so you can serve your guests who prefer more cooking the medium ribs, usually the outer ribs.

Accompaniments would include asparagus or broccoli, baked potato, and an oil-and-vinegar salad.

Lamb Shanks
serves 4

4 lamb shanks, about 1 pound each
1 large onion, chopped
2 stalks celery, strings peeled off, chopped
4 large carrots, peeled, cut length-wise in quarters, chopped
1 head of garlic, approximately 6–8 cloves, peeled and chopped
1 cup dry red wine
1 can chicken broth (14 ounces)
1 tablespoon dry thyme
2 bay leaves
1 teaspoon each kosher salt and coarse ground pepper
Extra virgin olive oil
Flour

Season the lamb shanks with salt and pepper at least ½ hour before cooking, but longer is better. Dredge the shanks in flour, shake off excess flour, and sear in olive oil in a Dutch oven, in batches if necessary. Remove the shanks and cook the onion, celery, and carrots in the oil. Return the shanks to the pot and cover with the wine, broth, thyme, and bay leaves.

Place the Dutch oven in a preheated 350° oven. Add broth or water if it dries out. Cook for 2–3 hours until the shanks are tender. Strain the braising liquid and defat the sauce. You can refrigerate at this point for up to 2 days and reheat on the stove when ready. Serve the shanks with the sauce on potatoes, rice, or pasta.

One of the advantages of this recipe is that you can make it ahead of time. Your friends will be amazed at how easy you make it look.

Poultry

Oven-baked Chicken Wings

2–4 pounds chicken wings
5 ounces Frank's Red-hot Original Sauce
1 stick butter or ½ cup extra virgin olive oil
Kosher salt and coarse ground black pepper

Melt the butter in a baking sheet with sides and add the jar of hot sauce. Cover the wings with the butter & hot sauce mixture as you add them to the baking sheet, rolling them so that they are fully coated. Lightly salt and pepper the wings.

Roast on the baking sheet in a 400° preheated oven for 45–60 minutes until they are brown. Turn the wings every 15 minutes. Enjoy!

Tips:
Line the baking sheet with aluminum foil to make cleanup a breeze or drain the oil and soak the pan in water and Cascade. For a crispier wing, sprinkle the oiled wings lightly with baking powder before baking. Experiment with different seasonings such as cayenne pepper or Rattlesnake Salt (page 55).

Faster Alternative: Parboil the wings and finish them on the grill. Parboil the wings for 7 minutes, drain in a colander, and dry with paper towels. Follow the above recipe for the sauce, brush the wings with the sauce and brown the wings on the grill.

The Buffalo Chicken Wing allegedly was invented in 1964 at the Anchor Bar in Buffalo, New York. There are an unlimited number of versions but the common side is celery with blue cheese or ranch dressing.

This version is included for its simplicity. From here you can embellish it with your favorite seasoning.

Butterflied Chicken
serves 4-6

1 chicken, 3–5 pounds
2 tablespoons extra virgin olive oil or canola oil
3–4 tablespoons Savory Grilling Rub (page 69) or 1 teaspoon each cumin and oregano with ½ teaspoon each kosher salt and coarse ground pepper

Cut the backbone out of the chicken. Freeze the backbone, the neck and the last one or two pieces of the wings in tightly wrapped plastic to make broth another day. Don't refrigerate it; you'll forget, and you can always start broth with a frozen backbone. Place the chicken skin- side up in a roasting pan and press the breast until it cracks and flattens. Coat the chicken with the oil and don't worry if some is left in the pan. Wash your hands, often, when you are preparing chicken.

Preheat the oven to 425° and cover both sides of the chicken with the Rub. Place the pan of chicken in the oven for about 1 hour (or until 165°).

Remove the chicken to a platter and allow it to rest at least 5 minutes before carving.

Grilling option: Cook the chicken on the grill at medium-high heat with the lid closed for about 1 hour (or until 165°). You can start the chicken skin-side down and turn it 10 minutes later to ensure the skin gets browned.

If you are serving 8 or more, you will need at least 2 chickens.

There are other names for Butterflied Chicken: Leaping Frog Chicken or Spatchcock Chicken. The result and the technique are the same. It is indeed just good food.

If you roast a whole chicken, the legs are likely to dry out. Butterflied Chicken is easier to carve and is more moist than cooking pieces. Why did it take us so long to figure this out?

Simply Baked Chicken
serves 4

1 chicken, cut up, or 4 chicken quarters
Extra virgin olive oil
Thyme for Salt or your favorite spice combination

Preheat the oven to 425°. Line a baking sheet with aluminum foil and oil the foil before adding the chicken. Spread the chicken out on the foil and coat the chicken with oil. Sprinkle the chicken with Thyme for Salt or your favorite spices.

Bake the chicken, skin side up, for 60 minutes, more or less, until the chicken has reached 165°.

Serve immediately or keep the chicken warm until ready to serve.

Background: This is a good recipe for anyone just learning to cook. It was very helpful in my first apartment in law school. Fortunately, the year before I had been an intern in Jerry Ford's office when he was minority leader of the U.S. House of Representatives. One of the very important things we did was provide constituents with the Congressional Cookbook. As a result, I got one for myself and I had more than Simply Baked Chicken for law school dinners!

The simplest recipe ever, right?

This seems too good to be true. It is a great last-minute solution to "What's for dinner?"

It was a favorite of our father on Friday nights when we were in school. It was proof (kind of) he could cook. All it took to be complete was a simple salad and French bread. Dessert: ice cream and a cookie.

Roast Lemon Chicken
serves 4-8

1 chicken, 4–7 pounds
2 lemons
4–5 cloves garlic
1 handful fresh rosemary, preferably on the stems.
Kosher salt and coarse ground pepper

Preheat the oven to 450°. Wash the chicken and rub the inside with salt and pepper. Squeeze 1 lemon inside the chicken so that it does not run out. Add the fresh rosemary and garlic to the inside of the chicken. Squeeze 1 lemon on the outside of the chicken and salt and pepper the outside.

Cook the chicken 1 hour for a 4-pound chicken and 1 hour and 15 minutes for a 6-pound chicken. Do not open the oven door while the chicken is roasting, not even once! Be patient, it will be worth it! Remove the chicken from the oven and put it on a platter to rest for 10 minutes.

Meanwhile, create a sauce for the chicken or potatoes by spooning off the fat from the pan and adding either a small can of chicken broth (14.5 ounces) or water. You may need flour to thicken. Whisk the sauce with a little heat on the stove and strain into a gravy boat. There should be plenty of salt and pepper from the chicken. Carve the chicken, cutting off the legs, thighs, and wings and finally slice the chicken breast. Serve proudly and do not tell anyone how easy it was.

The story behind this easy recipe is a little surprising. It was a specialty of the actor David Niven. He passed it on to Paula Perlini, an interior designer of some renown in New York and its vicinity. Paula passed it on to my wife June, while she was working at the Florence Griswold Museum in Old Lyme, Connecticut.

Almost everyone who makes it, claims it. You can too, unless you call it Chicken á la Niven or Chicken á la Perlini. Or Chicken á la June!

Chicken á la King
serves 8

½ pound button mushrooms, cleaned and chopped or sliced
1 green pepper, chopped (or a small can, 4 ounces, green chillies)
1 jar (5 ounces) pimentos, chopped and drained (or 1 red pepper, chopped)
1 medium onion, chopped fine
4 tablespoons (½ stick) butter
¼ -⅓ cup flour
1 cup milk, Half and Half, or fat-free Half and Half
1 cup chicken broth
2 cups (maybe more) cooked chicken or turkey, chopped
1 teaspoon sugar
½ teaspoon kosher salt
¼ teaspoon coarse ground black pepper
¼ teaspoon turmeric

Sauté the mushrooms, green pepper, pimentos, and onion in the butter until the onion is translucent and the mushrooms and pepper are soft. Add the flour and while stirring add the milk and broth. Finally, add the seasonings and cook 15–30 minutes at a simmer.

Serve over puff pastry cups or toast.

What to do with all that leftover Thanksgiving turkey? This is part of our answer. We also love sandwiches and turkey chili.

Chili is a great way to use the carcass to create a wonderful stock! You need one cup of that stock here. Simply boil the carcass in a quart or two of water with some chopped onions, celery, and carrots, or just the water. Rescue the chicken meat for the chili and Chicken á la King, strain the stock, and discard the rest.

This was a favorite of my father who would order it for Dutch treat get togethers with his friends. I come by this "just good food" way quite naturally.

Skillet Chicken
serves 8

3 chicken breast halves, sliced horizontally to create pieces
4 boneless chicken thighs, cut into the same size as the breasts
½ cup flour
1 tablespoon each, kosher salt and coarse ground pepper
Extra virgin olive oil
1 large onion, chopped
1 pound mushrooms, washed, stemmed, and cut in half or sliced
1–2 pounds small potatoes, peeled slightly and cut up as necessary
2 cups cherry tomatoes, cut in half
1 can (14 ounces) chicken broth
1 cup white wine (what you are drinking or dry vermouth)
Fresh parsley, chopped, or dried

Put flour, salt, and pepper in a dish and coat each slice of chicken on both sides. In a large frying pan, add enough olive oil to cover and heat on medium high. Add the chicken and sauté on both sides until browned, setting aside the finished pieces until the remaining ingredients are cooked.

Sauté the onion, mushrooms, potatoes, and finally the tomatoes. Add the broth and wine, reserving some to add to the leftover flour to create a roux which should also be added. Adjust the salt and pepper as needed. Cover with the chicken and bake at 375° for 45 minutes to an hour, removing the cover for the last 15 minutes. Top with parsley before serving.

Like other recipes in this book, Skillet Chicken can be prepared ahead and refrigerated until it is time to put in the oven. It will require a little longer to cook because it is cold.

I made this for a small gathering of friends, including June, before we married. I invited the same group two weeks later for the Super Bowl with an additional couple. June requested the Skillet Chicken. About a year later June and I got engaged, and I like to think it wasn't just because of the Skillet Chicken!

Saltimbocca Chicken
serves 8

4 chicken breast halves, sliced horizontally to create 8 pieces
½ cup flour
1 tablespoon each, kosher salt and coarse ground pepper
Extra virgin olive oil
8 thin slices prosciutto
8 thin slices Swiss cheese
1 can (14 ounces) chicken broth
¼ cup white wine (dry vermouth will do)
Fresh parsley, chopped, or dried

Put flour, salt, and pepper in a dish and coat each slice of chicken on both sides. In a large frying pan, add enough olive oil to cover and heat on medium high. Add the chicken and sauté on both sides until browned, then set aside until all the chicken has been cooked.

Arrange the chicken in an oven-proof dish and cover each piece of chicken with a slice of prosciutto and a slice of cheese. Then deglaze the pan with the wine and add enough of the remaining flour to thicken the sauce after adding the broth. Bring to a boil, cook down, and scrape the residue in the pan to combine into a sauce. Add the sauce to the baking dish.

The dish may be covered with plastic wrap and put in the refrigerator. Remove from the refrigerator and cook in a preheated 375° oven, about 30–45 minutes, until the cheese bubbles. The chicken should reach an internal temperature of 165°. Top with parsley before serving.

I included a Veal Scaloppine recipe in Just Good Food for Good Friends *which several friends said was what they knew as Saltimbocca. In other words, this is the Veal Scaloppine recipe using chicken.*

Usually, the chicken or veal is pounded, but the the chicken tends to dry out. For veal, which is more chewy, the pounding helps.

Veal is harder to find, and once you try this you may never go back.

Seafood

Mussels in White Wine
serves 2 for dinner or 4-8 for an appetizer

2 pounds cultivated mussels
¼ cup all purpose flour
2 tablespoons butter
2 tablespoons extra virgin olive oil
4–5 shallots, chopped
3 cloves garlic, chopped fine
½ cup drained plum tomatoes, chopped, or 1 tablespoon Dijon mustard, depending on whether you want a tomato or Dijon base
¼ cup chopped flat-leaf parsley or 1 tablespoon dried
1 tablespoon thyme leaves or 1 teaspoon dried
1 cup white wine (what you are drinking or dry vermouth)
2 teaspoons kosher salt + 1 teaspoon coarse ground black pepper
1 baguette

Clean the mussels by putting them in a bowl with 6 cups of cold water and the flour. Soak for 30 minutes to allow the mussels to release any sand. Drain and remove the beard from each mussel with your fingers. Dispose of any mussels that are not tightly closed.

Heat the butter, olive oil, shallots, and garlic in a non-aluminum pot until they are translucent. Add the tomatoes (or Dijon), spices, and wine and bring to a boil. Add the mussels and stir, cover, and cook over medium heat 8–10 minutes until they open, discarding any that have not opened. If the heat is too high, you may need to stir or shake the pot to be sure they do not burn on the bottom.

Pour the mussels and broth into a large bowl and serve with roasted or toasted baguette slices to dip and eat with the mussels.

Soooo good! They are tender, sweet, and delicious!

This is a meal that we used to think was too complicated to make at home. Mussels are also easier to find now in most supermarkets. Surprisingly, they are one of the most reasonably priced seafoods.

It's actually more fun to eat them at home so you can simply "dig in!"

Sautéed Fish
serves 4

4 servings of fish filets, preferably fresh, your choice of what looks best: flounder, cod, halibut, whitefish, etc.
Flour, cornmeal, breadcrumbs, or none at all
Extra virgin olive oil or canola oil
Butter, wedges of lemon, and fresh parsley
Kosher salt and coarse ground black or white pepper (Thyme for Salt or Tuscan Rosemary Salt works well with fish, recipes found in the Salts & Sauces section)

Remove the fish from the refrigerator 15 minutes before cooking. Select a thick frying pan that will accommodate all of the fish. Season the fish with salt and pepper and dip in the flour. Heat the pan until medium hot, add the oil to lightly coat the pan, and then add the fish skin-side down if you chose fish with skin.

Heat (you may need to increase the heat) until the edges of the fish start to turn white. Flip the fish and add butter to the pan. Continue cooking, but if the filet is thin, turn off the heat, allowing the pan to do its thing. **Note:** If you chose a thick filet, place the pan in a preheated 400° oven to finish.

The cooking time should be about 6 minutes, up to 10–15 minutes depending on the thickness of the filet. Don't overcook! That's an order. Remove the fish, squeeze a little lemon in the oil, stir the sauce and add to the fish. Serve with wedges of lemon and chopped parsley.

When you see beautiful fish at your favorite fish market, there is often that hesitation as you think about how you're going to cook it. None of these recipes require anything special. You are ready!

Alternative 1: Broiler
Heat the broiler and add a thick roasting pan to the broiler until hot. Add the oil and follow the basic recipe using the broiler.

Alternative 2: Grill
Heat up a grill pan on your grill. Follow the basic recipe but drizzle the fish with oil before placing it on the grill pan. Add the butter to the fish at the very end and finish with lemon and parsley on your serving platter.

Fish Tacos & Slaw
serves 4

½ cup mayonnaise
4 teaspoons lime juice (juice from 2 limes)
1 or 2 dashes of Tabasco (or your favorite hot sauce)
½ teaspoon kosher salt and ¼ teaspoon coarse ground pepper
½ head cabbage, cored and sliced thin
1 onion sliced to match the cabbage

4 filets of an inexpensive white fish such as tilapia (total 1 pound)
3 tablespoons extra virgin olive oil
2 cloves garlic, minced
2 tablespoons smoked paprika or sweet paprika, your favorite
1½ tablespoons oregano
1½ teaspoons cumin, pepper flakes, lime zest, and kosher salt
½ teaspoon coarse ground black pepper
Your favorite taco shells

In a bowl, combine the first 4 ingredients and toss with the cabbage and onion. Refrigerate.

Combine the seasonings listed after the fish. Rinse and dry the fish then roll in the seasonings. Heat a frying pan to medium hot and add the oil to the pan. Sauté the seasoned fish 3–4 minutes a side. Warm the taco shells and add the fish and slaw. Top with fresh avocado, salsa, or salsa verde. Serve and enjoy!

The slaw can be made ahead and refrigerated. The fish can be made ahead and kept warm in the oven. Then all you need are guests!

This can also be an appetizer for informal gatherings without dinner.

Fishcakes
serves 4

½ pound leftover cooked fish or the same amount freshly sautéed
1–2 shallots, chopped fine
1–2 tablespoons red pepper, chopped fine
¼ cup panko breadcrumbs or grated boiled or baked potato
Kosher salt and coarse ground black pepper or Thyme for Salt or Tuscan Rosemary Salt (recipes in Salts & Sauces section)
1–2 tablespoons mayonnaise
1 egg white
Extra virgin olive oil

Break up the fish and mix with shallots, pepper, breadcrumbs, and seasoning. Add the egg white and mayonnaise and mix well. Using a large spoon or measuring cup create four equally sized patties. You can refrigerate the fish cakes at this point until you're ready to prepare dinner.

Heat a frying pan, large enough for all four fish cakes, to medium heat. Add oil to the pan and saute 3–4 minutes a side. Serve with a squeeze of lemon and freshly chopped parsley or perhaps a sauce like Comeback Sauce (page 59) or Cajun Dip (page 6).

You can serve the fishcakes on a heated bun, burger style, to keep it simple. Lettuce, tomato, and mayonnaise (or sauce) will make it deluxe!

It isn't unusual to have leftover fish as you try to gauge the appetites of your guests. What to do with the leftovers so that they aren't clearly leftovers any more? This is it!

You may even want to buy more fish than you need just so you can have fishcakes!

Lobster Tails
serves 2

2 lobster tails
Kosher salt and coarse ground pepper
2 tablespoons butter
1 tablespoon lemon juice

Wash the lobster tails and butterfly them by cutting them down the middle. Sprinkle with salt and pepper. Place the tails in a frying pan, cut side up, with a cover and ½ cup water for every two lobster tails. Bring to a boil and cook covered for 8 minutes.

Meanwhile, cook the butter over low heat in a small saucepan until melted. Let stand for several minutes and skim off the the froth and pour the butter into a small bowl, leaving behind the solids in the bottom of the pan. Add the lemon juice to the butter.

Serve the lobster meat with the clarified butter and lemon juice.

Opportunity: Lobster Rolls
Cut up the cooked lobster into bite-sized chunks and refrigerate. In a bowl, add 3 tablespoons mayonnaise, ¼ cup finely chopped celery (or less green onion), 2 teaspoons lemon juice, a dash of hot sauce, kosher salt, and ground black pepper. Adjust seasoning and mix in the lobster. Butter hot dog buns and heat, butter side down, in a frying pan with the cover on until lightly browned.

Serve the lobster mixture in the buns and top with some butter lettuce if desired. Enjoy!

This is the ultimate treat! You can do it for a lot less than a restaurant will charge. Once you prove you can do it, there is no reason not to.

While the recipe is for two, it is easily expanded to serve more, with a larger pan or pans. You will, of course, need more butter and lemon juice, using a small bowl for every two people, if you do not give each person his or her own.

Lobster makes a great dinner but the lobster rolls are also a treat and you don't have to go all the way to Maine to have them!

Shrimp and Grits
serves 4

1 cup stone-ground yellow or white grits
2 cups water
2 cups (at least) whole milk
½ teaspoon kosher salt
¼ teaspoon coarse ground black pepper

Heat the water and and pour the grits into the boiling water in a stream, stirring. Add the milk ¼ cup at a time until thick and all of the milk has been added. Be careful not to step away for too long or the bottom will scorch. You may need to add more milk if the dinner is delayed and you kept the heat on low. Of course a little grated extra-sharp cheddar cheese won't hurt.

1 pound shrimp, peeled and deveined
1 small onion, 1 red pepper, 1 green pepper (or jalapeno), chopped
½ pound andouille or other hot sausage, cut up (optional)
¼ teaspoon cayenne pepper (optional)
Extra virgin olive oil
1 can (14 ounce) chopped tomatoes
1 can (14 ounce) chicken broth
1 teaspoon seasoned salt or Thyme for Salt (page 54)

Sauté the onion and pepper in a little extra virgin olive oil (with the sausage if you are using it) and add the tomatoes and broth once the onion is translucent. Cook at least 15 minutes to reduce the liquid, then add the shrimp and seasonings and cook 5 minutes, until the shrimp are pink. Serve grits topped with the shrimp mixture; a large bowl for each serving works well. Top with parsley or chives or just dig in!

We have been going to Charleston since my brother (and editor) Steve moved there in the mid 1970s. For awhile, we thought this was the only local dish. Not true. But it seemed to be on every local restaurant's menu. Each said theirs was the best.

Coquilles St. Jacques
serves 6

18 sea scallops, the large ones (3 per person)
3 tablespoons butter, plus a little extra virgin olive oil as needed
3 shallots, chopped
¾ pound cremini, button, or other small mushrooms, cleaned, stemmed, and sliced thin
2–3 tablespoons flour or corn starch
¾ cup dry white wine (dry vermouth will do)
¾ cup heavy cream, more as needed
¼ teaspoon curry powder and/or thyme
½ teaspoon kosher salt
¼–½ teaspoon coarse ground black pepper
½ cup panko breadcrumbs
¼ pound grated Gruyère or Swiss cheese

Place 3 scallops (sauté them first if they are wet to get out the extra liquid) in six individual serving dishes or all in one baking dish (9 x 9 inch if smaller scallops, or 9 x 12 inch if larger). Sauté the shallots in the melted butter in a 2-quart saucepan until soft. Add the mushrooms and continue to cook until they are soft. Add flour or corn starch and stir, adding wine (and cooked scallop sauce if they were wet) to create a creamy sauce. Add the cream and spices and continue cooking until the sauce thickens.

Pour the mushroom sauce over the scallops. Mix the breadcrumbs and grated cheese and top the dishes. Refrigerate until dinner, then bake at 400° for 20 minutes in a preheated oven until bubbling.

This was a classic French appetizer, back in the day. Today it is too rich, so instead of 2 scallops for an appetizer, this is 3 scallops for dinner.

Serve with a tossed salad and baguette and, of course, some wonderful wine. A chardonnay from Burgundy would be perfect but another dry white wine will work, even a pinot noir would balance the flavors.

This is usually cooked in stages with the shallots and mushrooms cooked and added to the sauce. I wanted to see if it would work in one saucepan. It worked in a Just Good Food *kind of way. Julia Child might have objected, but fortunately she was nowhere to be seen.*

Salmon in Parchment

serves 4, maybe more

2 pounds fresh salmon, rinsed and dried
1 onion and 1 fennel bulb, each cut in half, and sliced ⅛-inch thick
1 tablespoon frond of the fennel, washed and chopped
1 tablespoon extra virgin olive oil
2 teaspoons dry thyme (2 tablespoons fresh thyme)
Juice from half a lemon and lemon zest
1 teaspoon kosher salt
½ teaspoon coarse ground black pepper

Sauté the onion and fennel in the olive oil until translucent but still firm. Add lemon juice, zest, thyme, salt, and pepper and cook slightly to reduce the liquid.

Place the salmon skin-side down on a large piece of parchment and cover with the onion-and-fennel mixture. Seal the parchment by folding over the long side of the salmon and then folding the ends like a birthday present.

Place the salmon package on a heated pan with sides (heat the pan 5 minutes in the oven) and cook 20 minutes in a 500° preheated oven.

The advantage of this recipe is that you can get the salmon package ready before the guests arrive. Place the package in the refrigerator if you're preparing way ahead. Place the pan in the oven while it is preheating and add 5 minutes to the cooking time to compensate for the cold fish.

Of course you don't have to limit this recipe to salmon, nor do you have to use fennel. Consider other vegetables like cauliflower, broccoli, zucchini, asparagus, etc. The onion will need sautéing as would cauliflower and broccoli, but zucchini and asparagus, depending on the thickness, should need very little.

Cod, Boursin Cheese, and Tomatoes
serves 4-6

2 pounds of cod filets
1 package Boursin cheese, 4–6 ounces, at room temperature
2 cans (15 ounces each) diced tomatoes with basil, garlic, and oregano, drained
Butter and/or extra virgin olive oil
Finely grated Parmesan or Gruyère cheese
Kosher salt and coarse ground pepper or Thyme for Salt (page 54)

Preheat the oven to 400°. Wash and dry the cod with a paper towel. Put the butter on the bottom of a baking pan or oven-proof frying pan and top with the cod and lightly salt and pepper. Spread the Boursin cheese over the cod and then add the drained tomatoes. Grate the Parmesan or Gruyère cheese lightly on top. Put the cod in the oven for 15–25 minutes, depending on the thickness.

You can prepare the cod for baking and refrigerate until you are ready to put it in the oven. It should take a little longer in the oven if it has been refrigerated. Serve with Brussels sprouts, roasted fennel, or fresh cooked summer vegetables.

Cod can use a little extra flavor and the Boursin is just the thing. No need for a sauce.

If you can't find the tomatoes with spices, you can cut up the tomatoes in a 28-ounce can and add your own spices. They are an important part of the flavor.

Pasta / Italian

Pasta Carbonara
serves 4

3 eggs, beaten lightly
¼ pound pancetta, guanciale, or bacon, chopped
1 medium onion, chopped, or 1 clove garlic, sliced
½ cup Pecorino Romano cheese, finely grated
1 cup Parmigiano-Reggiano cheese, finely grated
1 teaspoon coarse ground black pepper
¼ teaspoon kosher salt, or to taste
1 pound spaghetti

Remove the eggs from the refrigerator and set aside. Boil a 4–6 quart pot of water with 1 tablespoon of salt. Meanwhile, cook the pancetta over medium heat, stirring often, until crisp, and set aside. Cook the onion or garlic in the fat until it is very tender, stirring as needed. If using garlic, remove from the fat.

Add the spaghetti to the water and cook until al dente (cooked but still slightly firm). Lightly beat the eggs and add the cheese, pepper, and salt. Reserve a cup of the pasta water. Drain the spaghetti in a colander and add it to the pan of fat (and onion). Then toss the eggs and cheese into the spaghetti followed by just enough of the water to create a sauce.

Finally, add the pancetta, toss, and serve immediately. Save some cheese to sprinkle on top.

Ruth Reichl was interviewed about her compilation of the Gourmet cookbooks. She was asked what she fixed on the spur of the moment when she returned home with an anxious family waiting for dinner. This recipe was her answer.

I had long looked at carbonara recipes and wondered about the raw egg. Did it really cook in the hot pasta? It does! And it can be made in the spur of the moment. All you need is the pancetta or bacon (which can be kept in the freezer). You should have the rest of the ingredients for day-to-day cooking. If you don't have Pecorino, you can just use more Parmigiano-Reggiano. You may even prefer that since the Pecorino is very salty.

Guanciale is an Italian cured-meat product prepared from pork jowel and it is commonly used in carbonara recipes.

Pasta Primavera
serves 4

2 tablespoons extra virgin olive oil
½ large sweet onion or Vidalia onion, julienned
3 cloves garlic, peeled, julienned
4 medium carrots, cut in half, julienned
½ red pepper, cut into thin julienne (like a matchstick) slices
1 medium zucchini, cut in half, seeded, julienned
1 medium yellow squash, cut in half, seeded, julienned
1 teaspoon dried thyme, 1 teaspoon coarse ground black pepper, and ½ teaspoon kosher salt
¼–½ cup heavy cream
½ pound capellini pasta (angel hair)

Sauté the onion and garlic in a large pan, stirring until just before they are translucent. Add the carrots and red pepper and continue stirring and cooking. Boil a 4–6 quart pot of water with 1 tablespoon of salt.

Meanwhile, add the zucchini and yellow squash to the pan and cook until softened. Then add the spices and stir. Add the cream and stir, lowering the heat while you cook the pasta until al dente (cooked but still slightly firm). Reserve a cup of the pasta water. Drain the pasta in a colander, and add it to the pan of vegetables along with some of the pasta water if it is needed to create a saucy dish, but not too runny.

Serve on plates and top with grated Parmigiano-Reggiano.

We have all heard of the dish Pasta Primavera. Must be an old Italian dish? Nope. It was first introduced in New York City in the 1970s at the restaurant Le Cirque.

The origin of this recipe allows each chef to do their own thing and call it Pasta Primavera. This is my version. Have fun creating your own.

Try other vegetables cut into small pieces, like broccoli or cauliflower, thin asparagus, or peas. If you use broccoli or cauliflower you should blanche them first in boiling water, then immerse them in ice water well before you add them to the other vegetables. If you don't blanche them first they will take much longer to cook and there is not enough moisture to cook them properly.

Pesto Sauce
serves 4

2 large garlic cloves
⅓ cup pine nuts
½ teaspoon kosher salt
¼ teaspoon coarse ground black pepper
2 cups packed fresh (standard sweet) basil leaves
½ cup extra virgin olive oil
1 cup (or more) grated Parmigiano-Reggiano cheese
½ pound angel hair pasta (or your favorite pasta)

Put the garlic in a food processor and finely chop. Add the pine nuts, salt, and pepper and process. Then add the basil and process; with the processor running add the oil through the chute until reasonably smooth. Taste and add more salt or pepper as needed.

Boil a 4–6 quart pot of water with 1 tablespoon of salt. Add the pasta to the water and cook until al dente (cooked but still slightly firm). Reserve a cup of the pasta water. Put half of the pesto in a large bowl and add ¼ cup of the pasta water. Then drain the pasta and add the pasta to the pesto and toss. Add the remaining pesto, more pasta water if it seems dry, and toss with the cheese.

Serve with additional grated cheese on each serving. For an additional treat, add toasted walnuts and/or chopped sun-dried tomatoes just before tossing with the cheese.

This is so special at the end of a great summer season, but you don't have to wait for the end. You may have several "crops" during the summer. I prefer adding the cheese later but the more normal procedure is to add it with the basil.

If you refrigerate it, cover the pesto with plastic wrap in the container. You can refrigerate it for one week or freeze it for several months.

Pesto is also great on pizzas or sandwiches. Once it is in your repertoire, you will find more creative uses.

Eggplant Parmesan
serves 4

2 medium-to-large eggplants
Extra virgin olive oil
8 cloves garlic, minced
1 can (28 ounce) Italian plum tomatoes, drained, picked of skin, stems, and cores, and chopped
2 tablespoons tomato paste
2 teaspoons dried basil
1 teaspoon sugar (or 1 grated carrot)
½ teaspoon kosher salt & ¼ teaspoon coarse ground black pepper
½ pound mozzarella or Gruyère cheese, grated fine
¼ pound Parmigiano-Reggiano cheese, grated fine

Peel the eggplant if the skin is thick or if it is less than firm. Cut the eggplant into ¼-inch slices. Place on paper towels, sprinkle with salt and cover with more paper towels. After an hour or so, remove the towels and brush off the salt. Brush the olive oil and half of the garlic on the eggplant. Place the oiled eggplant on a baking tray and broil. After the eggplant looks cooked, about 15 minutes, flip and continue cooking so the second side looks as cooked as the first.

Meanwhile, sauté the remaining half of the garlic in oil and add the chopped tomatoes, tomato paste, and spices and cook until the sauce thickens, approximately 15 minutes. Put some oil in a baking dish and layer the sauce, eggplant, and cheese, at least two and perhaps three layers. Bake at 375° for 30 minutes.

To shorten the preparation time, make the sauce in advance or purchase a good marinara sauce.

The obvious alternative to eggplant is to slice chicken breasts horizontally. Dip in a beaten egg, then bread crumbs, and sauté. Layer the chicken with sauce and cheese and bake.

Shrimp and Caper Pasta
serves 4

2 pounds shrimp (approximately 25 per pound), shelled & deveined
¼ cup extra virgin olive oil
2 cloves garlic, minced
Juice of 1 large or 2 small lemons
2 tablespoons capers, drained and chopped
½ cup white wine (dry vermouth will do)
½ teaspoon kosher salt & ¼ teaspoon coarse ground black pepper
1 teaspoon dried thyme (1 tablespoon fresh)
1 pound pasta, your favorite
Parmigiano-Reggiano cheese, grated fine

Boil a 4–6 quart pot of water with 1 tablespoon of salt. Sauté the shrimp in the olive oil until it turns pink on one side. Add the garlic and continue cooking until both sides of the shrimp are pink. Add the lemon juice, capers, and wine and cook until a sauce is created. Salt and pepper the shrimp-and-caper sauce, adding the thyme before tasting to determine any adjustment.

Add the pasta to the water and cook until al dente (cooked but still slightly firm). Reserve a cup of the pasta water. The olive oil is critical to creating the sauce for the shrimp and pasta. If it is too dry, add some of the pasta water. Serve with the grated cheese on top.

I love recipes with ingredients I already have on hand. You don't already have a bag of shrimp in your freezer? This is one good reason to do so.

Of course, you can easily double this recipe but don't double the salt and pepper.

This is a great recipe for linguine if you enjoy wrapping it around your fork and stabbing a shrimp! If you opened white wine it will pair well with this dish.

Shrimp and Sausage Risotto
serves 8

2 tablespoons butter
1 tablespoon extra virgin olive oil
½ pound smoked Andouille sausage or other spicy smoked sausage, sliced thin
1 onion, chopped to provide ½ to 1 cup (though more won't hurt)
1 red pepper, chopped
1 jalapeno pepper, seeded and chopped
4 cloves garlic, chopped fine
2 cups Arborio rice
1 box (32 ounce) chicken broth, preferably low salt, heated with ½ cup white wine (dry vermouth will do)
1 pound button mushrooms, washed, stemmed, and sliced thin
2 pounds shrimp, shelled and deveined
½ teaspoon kosher salt
¼ teaspoon coarse ground black pepper
Grated Parmesan cheese

Melt the butter with the olive oil and add the sausage, onion, red and jalapeno pepper, and garlic. Cook until softened. Add the rice and cook 2–3 minutes to coat the rice. Add the hot broth and wine ½ cup at a time and cook until the stock is absorbed and the rice is tender and creamy, but still firm.

Meanwhile sauté the mushrooms in more olive oil and butter and then the shrimp, salt, and pepper. Cook until the shrimp turn pink. Add the mushrooms and shrimp to the rice and stir. Add Parmesan cheese before serving.

I wanted to make paella but I was enjoying the party and timing was crucial to get the crust. This was my solution to get the taste without the pressure.

You can do all but the shrimp and hold it there. Add the shrimp and then combine about 5 minutes later for a perfect paella-like dinner.

All you need to add is a great salad and bread.

Beef and Mushroom Pasta
serves 4

2 tablespoons extra virgin olive oil
2 cloves garlic, minced
1 large sweet onion, chopped
½ pound button mushrooms, sliced
1 pound beef tenderloin, cut into ¾-inch cubes
1 can (14.5 ounces) beef broth
1 teaspoon kosher salt, ½ teaspoon coarse ground black pepper or
    1 tablespoon Rattlesnake Salt (page 55)
½ pound egg noodles or fettuccine

Sauté the garlic and onion until translucent and add the mushrooms. Cook until soft but not browned, stirring so that everything is equally cooked. Season with some salt and pepper. You can hold the dish at this point until the guests are ready to eat. Meanwhile, boil a 4–6 quart pot of water with 1 tablespoon of salt.

Add the beef and sauté about 5 minutes over medium-high heat and season with the rest of the salt and pepper. Add the beef broth, preferably after reducing it slightly in a sauce pan. At the same time, cook the pasta. Reserve a cup of the pasta water. Drain the pasta and add to the beef and mushrooms. If it is too dry, add some of the pasta water.

You could use a less expensive cut of meat, but you'd have to cook it much longer to tenderize it. Of course with beef tenderloin it's fantastic, and it goes together quickly once you get the onions and mushrooms ready. It is simple but flavorful. Everyone will be impressed!

You could also serve it without noodles, but then you may want a starch to go with it.

Brunch

Almond Biscotti
serves 8, maybe

- 1¼ cups almonds, skinned and toasted
- 1¾ flour (all-purpose or unbleached)
- 2 teaspoons baking powder
- ¼ teaspoon kosher salt
- 1 cup sugar
- 4 tablespoons butter, melted
- 2 large eggs and 1 egg white for brushing the tops
- 1½ teaspoons almond extract
- 1 teaspoon vanilla extract

Preheat oven to 350°. Finely chop ¼ cup almonds and coarsely chop the remaining cup of almonds.

Combine the finely chopped almonds, flour, baking powder, and salt. Meanwhile, combine the sugar, melted butter, eggs, almond extract, and vanilla extract. Add the almond/flour mixture to the egg mixture and blend at low speed in a mixer.

Divide the batter in half and create 2 rectangles about 8 x 3 inches on sheets of parchment. Slice the rectangles in ¾-inch slices and spray or brush with oil and brush with the egg white. Bake approximately 35 minutes until lightly browned.

When you have overnight guests, coordinating breakfast for everyone can be challenging. Leave out some coffee, tea, and a batch of biscotti for the early risers and it won't matter what else you do. You will have happy campers!

Crunchy Granola
many breakfasts

5 cups old-fashioned rolled oats
2 cups pecans, roughly chopped
½ cup light or dark brown sugar, packed
¼ cup honey
¼ cup maple syrup
3 tablespoons coconut oil (or canola oil)
3 tablespoons water
1 teaspoon vanilla extract
1 teaspoon cinnamon
½ teaspoon kosher salt
½-1 cup dried cherries, raisons, cranberries, or Craisins

Put the oats and pecans in a large mixing bowl and set aside. Add all of the remaining ingredients (except the fruit) in a sauce pan, mix, and bring to a boil. Pour over the oats and pecans and mix thoroughly.

Line two baking pans with sides with parchment paper. Preheat the oven to 300° and place the racks on the top and bottom third of the oven. Split the oat/pecan mixture between the two pans and place them in the oven for approximately 1 hour, stirring at least once. Once the mixture is dried out, remove and allow to cool. Add the fruit and store in an airtight container in the refrigerator.

Serve with milk or yogurt or just dig in!

Of course, a yogurt and granola parfait with fresh strawberries or blueberries is a wonderful breakfast all alone or as a dessert after brunch.

Start and end with the granola and layer with yogurt and fruit in a glass, preferably with a stem. A wine glass will work just fine.

Deviled Eggs
makes 12 half eggs

6 large eggs (Note: Eggs fresh from the market are too fresh and will be hard to peel. This is the time to use your "oldest" eggs.)
2 teaspoons kosher salt

Put the eggs in a saucepan with enough water to cover by 2 inches. Add the salt and bring to a rolling boil. Turn off the heat and cover the pan for 10 minutes. Remove the pan and drain the hot water and cool the eggs with cold water, shaking them in the pan to gently crack them. When the eggs are cool, peel, cut in half on the long side, and add the yolks to a mixing bowl.

3 tablespoons mayonnaise
1 tablespoon heavy cream
1 teaspoon cider vinegar
½ teaspoon sugar
¼ teaspoon kosher salt
½ teaspoon each of thyme and tarragon (or chives in place of one)

Combine the above ingredients in the order listed in a small bowl and add the mixture to the yolks. Mix thoroughly with a fork to create a smooth mixture. Test the mixture and adjust with more mayonnaise or cream if it is dry. Salt or season to perfect the flavor. Use a teaspoon to fill the egg whites. Sprinkle with more herbs or parsley (fresh or dry) if you want to show off how good they are.

Deviled eggs were once a favorite at parties. Then we were told not to eat them because of cholesterol. Forget that! Eggs, in moderation, are now back. If you don't believe me, serve them at a party in hopes there will be leftovers. You should be so lucky!

There are now fancy ways to do deviled eggs, but this is "just good food" to coin a phrase. A pastry bag to fill the eggs will make them look prettier, but they won't taste better.

What's missing? Most basic deviled eggs have yellow mustard. You won't miss it. But if you do, feel free to add a tablespoon or less as you are perfecting the flavor.

Sausage Gravy
serves 4-8

1 pound bulk breakfast sausage
½-1 teaspoon coarse ground black pepper
Kosher salt & red pepper to taste (ground sage & fennel optional)
¼ cup flour (all-purpose or unbleached)
2½–3 cups whole milk or Half and Half

Cook the sausage in a cast-iron skillet or other heavy-bottomed skillet. Break up the sausage as it cooks with a wooden spoon until it is no longer pink. Taste the sausage and add the seasonings to get the desired result. Salt and pepper are a must and the sage and fennel are optional.

Sprinkle the flour over the sausage (a mesh kitchen strainer will help distribute it), cook and stir constantly until the flour is incorporated. Slowly add the milk, continuing to stir until the gravy gets thick and ready to serve with biscuits or toast. You may need more milk as the gravy will continue to thicken as it cooks. That's why the milk quantity is an approximation.

An enhancement (usually for brunch when the next meal is dinner) is a poached or fried egg on each serving.

This is one of those meals that I used to eat only when dining out. Why did I wait so long before trying to make it at home? I guess I thought there was some kind of magic required, but it's actually pretty simple.

The real challenge is to make the biscuits from scratch (page 115). Of course you can buy a tube and save a lot of work, but biscuits from scratch are such a treat!

A simple seasoning alternative is Tuscan Rosemary Salt (page 55).

A Mess for Breakfast
serves 2

1 sausage link, skin removed and chopped
4 redskin (or other small potatoes) or 1 medium Yukon Gold potato (russet would be fine)
2 thin slices of sweet onion, chopped
2 eggs
¼ cup grated cheddar cheese
Kosher salt and coarse ground black pepper to taste, about ¼ teaspoon of each

Boil the potatoes, let them cool, and chop them. Sauté the sausage and then add the potatoes and onion in that order. The potatoes should start to brown before adding the onion.

Lightly beat the eggs, add the salt and pepper, and beat again. When the potatoes and sausage are cooked and the onion is starting to brown, add the egg mixture and stir slightly. Top with the cheese and either treat it like an omelet and fold it over, allowing the cheese and eggs to finish cooking, or simply stir until it is all cooked. Serve and enjoy!

What more can you add? Red, green, or hot pepper, chopped, adds color and flavor. Use about the same amount as the onion and add it with the onion. Your favorite herbs, especially if they are in your garden. It is called "a mess" so use your imagination and create your own mess!

This is a great recipe for when you have guests for the weekend. Multiply to determine the right amount of ingredients for the number of guests. You may need less than 1 egg per person as the group increases in size.

We find that a little cheese is better than a lot, but you decide.

You may substitute ham, bacon, or bulk sausage for the link sausage. Bacon or bulk sausage may require cooking first, then draining the grease, before adding the potatoes and onion.

Tomato and Cheese Frittata
serves 4-6, maybe more

2 tablespoons extra virgin olive oil
1 medium onion, chopped (about 1 cup)
1½ cups cherry tomatoes, washed and stems removed
6 eggs
¼ cup whole milk, Half and Half, or heavy cream
½ teaspoon kosher salt
¼ teaspoon coarse ground black pepper
1 cup finely grated Parmesan cheese or ½ cup grated extra-sharp white cheddar cheese

Sauté the onion in a large oven-proof frying pan. Add the salt and pepper and cook until the onion is translucent. Add the tomatoes and continue cooking until the skins start to shrink.

Meanwhile, beat the eggs and milk and pour over the onion and tomatoes. Distribute the tomatoes and onion so that they are spread throughout the pan. Continue to heat and sprinkle the cheese on top. Cook the egg mixture on medium heat until the eggs start to set. Place the pan in a preheated 350° oven and cook until the eggs are fully set.

Serve hot or warm with bacon or sausage and toast or biscuits.

This is really just a starting point. You can use skinned, seeded, and chopped fresh tomato or substitute seeded and chopped zucchini or spinach.

Goat cheese, ricotta, or some of the Parmesan or cheddar can be mixed into the eggs. Crumbled and cooked sausage can replace the tomatoes.

In other words, make it your own!

Breakfast Hash
serves 2

1–2 tablespoons extra virgin olive oil
1 potato, medium to large, peeled and chopped
1 medium onion, chopped
½ red pepper, seeded and chopped
4 ounces of leftover beef brisket, or salmon, etc.
Kosher salt and coarse ground pepper to taste

Sauté the potato in a frying pan until it starts to brown. Add the onion and continue cooking until the onion is translucent. Add the red pepper and cook, and finally add the brisket (or other meat) to make the hash. Salt and pepper to taste.

Fry or poach an egg for each serving. Top each serving of hash with the egg.

I was trying to think of other uses for beef brisket when I remembered hash. It worked! Salmon works great, obviously corned beef, etc. Use your imagination. You might even come up with something you can claim is original!

Perfect for when you have guests because you can easily multiply the ingredients to fit the number of people showing up for this special breakfast.

French Toast

serves 4

1 teaspoon sugar
½ teaspoon cinnamon
Dash of kosher salt
2 eggs, lightly beaten
1 teaspoon vanilla
½ cup milk
4 slices bread, sliced a little thicker than for a sandwich, crusts removed if they are hard
1 tablespoon butter, divided into four pieces
Maple syrup

Mix together all the dry ingredients. Combine the eggs and vanilla into the dry ingredients and whisk until smooth. Add the milk and whisk again. Place the mixture in a pie or cake pan and soak each slice of bread, adding another and stacking the previous one on top. Turn them all and place the top on the bottom until all sides have been soaked.

Heat a large frying pan or pancake griddle until hot and place the pieces of butter where a piece of toast will fit. Allow the butter to melt and add the bread. Cook until each side is browned and serve with maple syrup that has been heated slightly in a sauce pan or microwave oven.

There are a lot of bread choices, but basically whatever you have on hand will do. Many people prefer a slightly sweetened bread like brioche or cinnamon bread, while others always use whole wheat because that is what they normally eat.

Stale bread works well, and it's an excuse to have French Toast or to make croutons. But don't feel like you need an excuse because this is a great way to start the day!

If you want to clean up while you're waiting for your guests, you can fry them on both sides and then finish them in the oven at 350°. If you have an oven-proof pan, then you don't need to use a baking dish.

Cheese Soufflé
serves 6-8

½ cup butter (1 stick)
½ cup flour (all-purpose or unbleached)
2 cups whole milk
½ teaspoon kosher salt
Dash of Tabasco sauce or generous pinch of cayenne pepper
2 cups of grated extra-sharp cheddar cheese (about ½ pound)
1½ teaspoons dry mustard
6 eggs, separated

Preheat oven to 375°. Grease a 2-quart souffle dish.

Melt butter over medium heat in a heavy-bottomed sauce pan. Stir in flour and cook for a minute, then gradually add milk, stirring constantly until the mixture is smooth.

Add salt and Tabasco and remove from the heat and add cheese until it is melted and combined by stirring constantly. Add mustard and egg yolks until light, stirring constantly. Beat the egg whites until they hold soft peaks, then gently fold in the cheese mixture.

Pour into the buttered souffle dish and bake at 375° for 15 minutes, then reduce the heat to 300° and continue baking for 40–50 minutes. Serve a little bit of the crust with each serving.

This was a favorite of ours many years ago. Then we got concerned about our health. We finally looked at the ingredients and decided that it's not that bad.

A great way to show off what you can do!

Sour Cream Pancakes

serves 4

1 cup flour (all-purpose or unbleached)
1 tablespoon sugar
1 teaspoon baking soda
½ teaspoon kosher salt
½ cup sour cream
½ cup whole milk
2 large eggs
2 tablespoons melted butter or extra virgin olive oil
Maple syrup

Combine the dry ingredients and set aside. Combine the wet ingredients and whisk them into the dry ingredients.

Heat the griddle and melt a little butter or extra virgin olive oil on the surface. Wipe it down and spoon the the batter onto the griddle in your preferred pancake size. Heat until the pancakes bubble and then flip. Cook approximately the same time as the first side. Serve with heated maple syrup.

Pancakes are the medium that allows us to enjoy maple syrup. You want a simple soft pancake? This is it!

There is no better excuse to have a little sugar and a little protein, so that you're ready for the day.

If you have sour cream on hand, this is a great use for it. Greek yogurt will also work.

Johnnycakes
serves 4

1 beaten egg
½ cup milk
½ cup water
1 tablespoon melted lard or extra virgin olive oil
½ teaspoon kosher salt
1 cup cornmeal
Maple syrup

Mix the first four ingredients and then mix the salt and cornmeal and mix them together. Allow the batter to rest for at least 10 minutes before frying. It will take approximately ¼ cup of the batter for a Johnnycake.

Heat a griddle or frying pan with a little butter in the bottom. Add the batter for each Johnnycake and cook on each side until nicely browned.

Serve with butter and slightly warmed maple syrup.

Johnnycakes are thought to have originated with the Native Americans. They are a cross between pancakes and cornbread. There are many variations from all over the Americas and the Caribbean, but I love the simplicity of this one.

It took some trial and error to figure this out, but it was worth it. This is truly just good food.

Bread and Sandwiches

Hot French Bread With Herbs
serves 8

1 baguette, cut in half lengthwise
4 tablespoons (½ stick) butter at room temperature
1 clove of garlic, minced
1 teaspoon dried thyme (or 1 tablespoon fresh)
1 teaspoon dried savory (or 1 tablespoon fresh)
½ teaspoon coarse ground black pepper
½ teaspoon kosher salt

Preheat oven to 400°. Combine the butter and each of the next ingredients in the order listed. Spread the butter mixture on the bread and set it aside until you're close to dinnertime. Bake, butter-side up, for 10–15 minutes. Put the two half-loaves back together then slice and serve immediately after removing from the oven.

Tip for hot bread during dinner:
Before you bake the bread, put the two half-loaves back together and cut in half widthwise. Put the top and bottom of one half in the oven when you're close to dinnertime. Put the other half in the oven when you're serving dinner. Voila, a second piece of hot bread while you're eating dinner. It doesn't get much better than that!

The advantage of cooking the half-loaves cut-side up is that all of the butter melts into the bread and not on the pan. The less-butter alternative is to cook them cut-side down. You'll lose some of the butter, but they will still get brown.

This is great for a thin French baguette, but it works for any French bread. You may need more butter for a thicker baguette.

Biscuits
serves 8, barely

2 cups flour (all-purpose or unbleached), a premium brand
3 teaspoons baking powder (or make it fresh, see recipe below)
1¼ teaspoons kosher salt
4 tablespoons lard or cold butter
⅔ cup buttermilk
2 tablespoons melted butter

Preheat oven to 500°. Combine the flour, baking powder, and salt. Cut the lard into the flour mixture with your hands until the lard is in small flour-covered pieces. Add the buttermilk and stir with a wooden spoon into a ball. Place the ball on a floured board and press and roll out into a circle about ½-inch thick. Cut biscuits with a round cookie cutter or a sharp-edged round glass without twisting.

Bake on a greased cookie sheet (or parchment-covered cookie sheet), close together but not touching, until browned, about 10–12 minutes. Brush the top of the biscuits with melted butter.

Fresh Baking Powder option:
Combine ¼ cup cream of tartar and 2 tablespoons baking soda and sift 3 times. Store in a glass-covered jar in a dark cupboard for up to 6 weeks. Why? Commercial baking powders have chemical additives that leave an aftertaste and a biscuit needs the best ingredients you can find.

Once you get the hang of it, these are a snap. Why buy frozen when you already have the ingredients? Save the freezer for better things!

You can cut the recipe in half to serve two or four. However, the leftovers are so good you may want to stick to the full recipe.

Split a biscuit in half, lightly butter each half, and broil until the butter is melted and the biscuit is starting to brown. Delicious!

Cranberry Nut Bread
serves about 8

2 cups flour (all-purpose or unbleached), sifted
1 cup sugar
1½ teaspoons baking powder
1 teaspoon kosher salt
½ teaspoon baking soda
4 tablespoons butter
1 egg, well beaten
¾ cup strained orange juice
1 tablespoon grated orange peel
1 cup fresh or frozen cranberries, coarsely chopped
½ cup chopped walnuts or pecans

Preheat oven to 350°. Grease and flour a 9 x 5 inch loaf pan. Sift dry ingredients into a large bowl. Cut the butter into the flour mixture. Combine the egg, orange juice, and orange peel and add to the dry ingredients, mixing to just moisten. Fold in the berries and nuts and turn into the pan.

Bake approximately 1 hour until a toothpick inserted into the center comes out clean. Cool on a wire rack before removing it from the pan, then place on the rack to cool further. Wrap and store overnight to allow the flavors to develop.

This is a great recipe for your family, but it is also wonderful for friends who need a thoughtful gift. They may even ask for the recipe!

If you have leftover cranberries from Thanksgiving, they can be frozen and used later. Perfect recipe if you're looking for a healthier treat to make around the holidays.

If you can't wait until tomorrow to try it, slice off a piece and wrap up the rest. I don't blame you!

Blueberry Cornmeal Coffee Cake
serves 8-12

½ cup unsalted butter, softened
1 cup sugar (plus ¼ cup to sprinkle on top)
2 large eggs
1 tablespoon lemon zest (1 large or 2 small lemons)
1½ cups flour (all-purpose or unbleached)
½ cup medium-grind yellow cornmeal
2 teaspoons baking powder
½ teaspoon baking soda
½ teaspoon kosher salt
¾ cup buttermilk (or ¾ cup whole milk & 1 tablespoon lemon juice)
1½ cups fresh blueberries (approximately 7 ounces)

Preheat oven to 350° and butter an 8-inch springform pan. Cream butter and sugar about 2 minutes, adding 1 egg at a time at the end. Add the lemon zest to the creamed butter.

Stir together the flour, cornmeal, baking powder, baking soda, and salt and add to the butter, alternating with the buttermilk, beating on low speed. Add the blueberries and stir to combine.

Pour the batter into the buttered pan, sprinkle with the ¼ cup sugar and bake 45–50 minutes until lightly browned and the cake starts to pull away from the sides and the top springs back when pressed.

Cool 10 minutes and serve warm or at room temperature.

Blueberries used to have a very short season and it was a challenge to fit in all of my favorite recipes. No more! Now this can be a regular addition to breakfast or brunch.

It's also a delightful finish to a special lunch or as the feature during an afternoon bridge game. However, it might be gone by the time lunch rolls around!

Egg Salad Sandwiches
Serves 4

2 tablespoons finely chopped onion
1 tablespoon finely chopped celery (optional)
3 tablespoons mayonnaise
2 teaspoons Dijon mustard
4 hardboiled eggs (see page 104), peeled and chopped
¼ teaspoon coarse ground pepper
Kosher salt to taste

Mix the onion, celery if using, mayonnaise, and mustard. Add the chopped eggs and mix. Salt and pepper and mix lightly.

Serve on bread or toast with sliced tomato and lettuce.

Do you need an emergency lunch? I have you covered. Serve this, and your friends will think you planned it.

Tuna Salad Sandwiches
serves 2, maybe more

1 can (5 ounce) tuna in olive oil
1 hardboiled egg (optional)
⅓-½ cup celery, strings removed and chopped fine
⅓-½ cup sweet onion, chopped fine
2 tablespoons mayonnaise
Juice of 1 wedge of lemon
2 tablespoons red pepper, chopped (optional)

Drain the olive oil out of the tuna using a strainer while you chop the egg, celery, and onion. Combine them all with a fork so that they are nicely mixed. Add the mayonnaise and lemon juice and lightly toss with the fork.

Now comes the creative part of this sandwich. What do you love? Toast, bread, roll, lettuce and tomato? My recommendation is thinly sliced, really good bread toasted, with lettuce and tomato.

A favorite choice is a soft dinner roll, cut in half, buttered, and then broiled until slightly brown. Put tuna on one half and cheddar cheese on the other half, and broil until the cheese is melted and the tuna is hot. Put the two pieces together to make a sandwich and enjoy! If you prefer your tuna cool, broil only the cheese half; either way it is a treat. Of course, buttering the roll is not necessary.

Of course you can use tuna in water, but I think the tuna in olive oil tastes better.

Is 2 tablespoons of mayonnaise enough? It is the unhealthy part of this sandwich because 1 tablespoon has 90 calories, and they are all fat. Maybe you can live without it, or use light mayonnaise. However, most tuna salad recipes use a lot more.

Chicken Salad Sandwiches
serves 2-4

1 to 2 pounds cooked, chopped chicken
¼ to ⅓ cup mayonnaise
2 tablespoons sour cream or Greek yogurt
½ small lemon or ¼ regular lemon
½ teaspoon Dijon mustard
1 teaspoon dried tarragon
½ teaspoon kosher salt
¼ teaspoon coarse ground pepper
1 rib celery, strings removed and chopped into a ¼ inch dice
⅓ cup sweet onion or scallions, chopped fine
¼ cup toasted English walnuts or pecans (optional), broken into pieces
¼ cup dried cherries, cut up (optional)

In a bowl, combine the mayonnaise, sour cream or yogurt, lemon juice, and Dijon mustard, whisk to create a smooth sauce. Add the tarragon, salt and pepper and taste to adjust the flavors if necessary. Add the chicken, celery, and onion and fold gently to combine. Before serving, fold in the nuts if you are including them.

Serve the chicken salad on fresh bread or toast. Lettuce and tomato will complete the package, but are not necessary. Of course, chicken salad on a bed of lettuce with or without a vinaigrette dressing is also excellent.

We always need creative ways to use leftover chicken or turkey. Once you have mastered this, you will want to make extra chicken to ensure that you will have leftovers.

Poached chicken breast is even better for chicken salad and can be prepared in a matter of minutes. If you have my first cookbook, Just Good Food for Good Friends, *the recipe is on page 104.*

Mexi Chili Dogs
serves 8, maybe more

2 ½ pounds ground beef
3 tablespoons dried minced onion
1 can (28 ounce) tomato puree
1 tablespoon celery seed
1 tablespoon kosher salt
1 teaspoon chili powder
½ teaspoon course ground black pepper
¼ teaspoon cayenne pepper
Hot dogs and buns

Preheat oven to 275°. Sauté the ground beef in a skillet or Dutch oven with a cover until it starts to turn gray. Add the dried minced onion and continue to cook. Drain the fat and add the tomato puree and seasonings and cook 15 minutes. Cover and cook in the oven for 3 hours, more or less. Stir every 30 minutes or so until the seasonings and flavors meld into the Mexi Chili sauce.

Boil, steam, or grill hot dogs and heat hot dog buns. Offer the chili sauce for your guests to top their hot dogs.

Complete the party with coleslaw or potato salad and a very cold drink!

You can, of course, use the sauce for a "Sloppy Joe" served on a warm bun. In fact, you may want to do that to taste the sauce before serving the chili dogs.

This recipe came from my wife June, who misses the neighborhood root beer stand in Valparaiso, Indiana. Her mother was able to get the recipe from the retired owner who first had to cut it down from 20 pounds of ground beef.

The secret is the long cooking time in the oven which allows the flavors to come together.

Beef Brisket Sandwiches
serves 8-12

1 4–5 pound beef brisket
2 cloves garlic, minced
Barbecue Sauce (page 69), or your favorite
3–4 tablespoons of Savory Grilling Rub (page 69) or use the ingredients for Rib Rub substituting 1 teaspoon for ¼ cup, ½ teaspoon for 1 tablespoon, and ¼ teaspoon for 1 teaspoon

Preheat oven to 225°. Rub the brisket with the minced garlic on all sides. Then rub the brisket with the Savory Grilling Rub on all sides. Place the brisket fat-side up on a heavy piece of aluminum foil cut large enough so that it will wrap the brisket completely. Wrap tightly and transfer to a shallow roasting pan.

Place the brisket in the oven for 8 hours until the brisket is tender. Remove the fat, preserve the juice, and incorporate the juice in the cut-up brisket. Serve hot or cold on bread or rolls with Barbecue Sauce if needed.

For warm, crisp rolls, cut in half and butter each cut-side. Heat cut-side down in a covered frying pan or on a baking sheet covered in foil in a 300° oven until nicely browned.

My friend and colleague Fred Sytsma had saved a version of this recipe for about 30 years. When I needed a great sandwich for a large group, he searched his records and found it.

We had 10 for a casual gathering and a 4-pound brisket. I put it in the oven in the morning and never opened the oven until dinner. I did have a back-up plan. I knew I could cut it up and heat it covered in sauce if it still needed cooking. No problem. No leftovers either.

If there are leftovers (unlikely), I package 4-6 ounces of brisket in plastic wrap and freeze it for future sandwiches. A package will serve two adults, not two teenage athletes!

Avocado Toast
<small>serves 1–2 per avocado</small>

1 avocado cut in half, cut crosswise both ways, and spooned into a bowl
Juice of ¼ lemon
1–2 tablespoons red onion (or sweet, white, or green), sliced thin and chopped fine
2 tablespoons chopped tomato
¼ teaspoon each kosher salt and coarse ground pepper
1 or 2 slices of toast

This is a recipe for which precise directions are difficult. Each of the ingredients are approximate. The size of the avocado will determine the amounts for the other ingredients.

Mix and mash the ingredients to the consistency you prefer. Taste to determine if any ingredient should be increased to achieve your desired result. Spread on toast and enjoy!

Additions:
There are all sorts of additions that can embellish Avocado Toast: sliced radishes, crisp bacon, hard-boiled egg sliced or chopped, or a soft-boiled or fried egg on top.

This was one of those recipes I avoided because it looked like a challenge. My other cop-out was that it would take too long. Neither are true, it's easy and it takes less than 10 minutes to make. It's also the perfect use for an avocado that's getting too soft.

It's a great snack because it leaves you with a full feeling so you are less likely to eat junk!

Moreover, avocados provide the good fat, monounsaturated fat, as well as plenty of other vitamins we need.

Philly Sandwich
1 sandwich

Multiply the ingredients for the number of people:
Extra virgin olive oil
¼ white onion, sliced thin
¼ red pepper, sliced thin
½ jalapeno pepper, seeded and sliced thin
3 large button mushrooms, sliced thin
2 ounces beef steak, sirloin or your choice, sliced thin
½ teaspoon each kosher salt and coarse ground black pepper, or 1 teaspoon Savory Grilling Rub (page 69), or 1 teaspoon Rattlesnake Salt (page 55)
2 ounces, more or less, grated cheddar or Swiss cheese
1 hoagy roll, buttered and browned on the cut sides

Choose a frying pan large enough for the number of sandwiches you will be making. Sauté the onion in some olive oil until it is soft and translucent. Add the peppers and mushrooms and continue cooking. Add the thinly sliced beef and cook until it starts to brown, coating with the salt and pepper. Butter the cut sides of the rolls and brown them.

Place the cooked mixture on the roll and top with the grated cheese, or add the cheese to the meat mixture in the pan just before placing on the roll.

There are gatherings that just seem to call for a procession of Philly Sandwiches as fast as you can make them. The first step is to get ahead of the procession. Prepare the onion, peppers, and mushrooms in bulk and separately cook the steak in batches.

Of course, making 2 or 4 for a gathering works well and you can join the party. It could be a family specialty.

I had a Philly Sandwich once in Philadelphia with Velveeta cheese, so use whatever sounds good to you!

Desserts

Double Chocolate Brownies
serves 8

½ pound butter (2 sticks)
4 ounces unsweetened chocolate
4 ounces semi-sweet or bittersweet chocolate
1½ cups sugar
1 teaspoon kosher salt
4 large eggs
2 teaspoons vanilla extract
1 cup flour (all-purpose or unbleached)

Preheat oven to 350°. Melt the chocolate and butter. Mix the sugar and salt and add to the butter mixture, beating until light and fully blended. Add one egg at a time and beat along with the vanilla.

Fold in the flour and mix thoroughly. Butter an 8 x 8 or 9 x 9 inch baking pan. Pour the batter into the pan and spread it out evenly.

Bake for 35 minutes until it pulls away from the sides and is no longer runny. Don't overcook as dried-out brownies have to be eaten immediately, probably with vanilla ice cream.

Alternative: Sprinkle ½ cup chopped almonds and ½ of the kosher salt on top of the batter in the pan before baking.

The first time I made these brownies, I looked expectantly for a report. The response: Over the top! Once they had cooled, they were the perfect picker-upper, when no one was looking.

Double Chocolate Pudding
serves 8, barely

½ cup sugar
¼ cup cocoa powder, preferably Ghirardelli unsweetened
3 tablespoons corn starch
Pinch of salt
2 cups whole milk
2 chicken eggs or 1 duck egg
2 ounces unsweetened baking chocolate, preferably Ghirardelli 100% cacao, chopped fine

Mix the first four dry ingredients in a mixing bowl and set aside. Heat the milk in a quart saucepan until just prior to a boil. A film will start to develop on top. Meanwhile, beat the eggs and add them to the cocoa sugar mixture, beating so that they are combined. Add the hot milk in a stream, continuing to beat, and return the hot mixture to the saucepan. Heat and stir as the mixture thickens.

Once the chocolate is thick and you know it is pudding, add the chopped baking chocolate, continuing to stir until it is melted and an integral part of the mixture. It is now Double Chocolate Pudding! Pour into a bread-loaf pan or separate ramekins.

Cover the pudding with plastic wrap tight to the surface of the pudding to prevent a film on top. Refrigerate and enjoy when the time is right!

I'm sure you have made pudding from a store-bought mix. Have you ever made it from scratch? Didn't think you could? Now you can!

It may become a regular. It is that good. It has become a regular for us. Once you get the drill down, it is easy.

Strawberry Shortcake
serves 8

2 cups flour (all-purpose or unbleached), sifted
2 tablespoons sugar, plus extra when baking
1 tablespoon baking powder
1 teaspoon kosher salt
4 tablespoons butter (½ stick), plus extra when baking
⅔ cup whole milk
2–4 cups strawberries

Preheat oven to 400°. Combine the dry ingredients in a bowl. Cut in the butter with a pastry utensil or two knives. Mix with the milk until a soft dough is created.

Butter a 9-inch cake pan or baking dish and spread the dough evenly inside the pan. Brush with melted butter and sprinkle a tablespoon of sugar over the top. Bake for 20 minutes until lightly browned.

Wash and slice strawberries. Cut shortcake into slices and serve with strawberries and a little whipped cream or vanilla ice cream.

This is an old-time family recipe. It was used by my grandmother, Lena Chamberlain, at Point Nipigon Resort Club. She ran the Inn that my grandfather, Glenn R. Chamberlain, had built at the resort.

The southern way to serve is to cut each piece in half horizontally, butter in between, and place on a cookie sheet in a 250° oven until the butter and the shortcake are warm but the butter is not melted.

Panettone Bread Pudding
serves 4-8

3 eggs
1 egg yolk
1 teaspoon vanilla extract
½ cup sugar
2 cups heavy cream or Half and Half
Pinch of kosher salt
Panettone bread, 5–6 cups in 1–2 inch cubes, dark crust removed (out of Panettone season, challah or brioche will work well and some dried cherries will provide the zip)

Combine the eggs, yolk, vanilla, and sugar. Add the cream and heat until it thickens to create a custard. Set aside in the refrigerator until you are ready to bake the pudding.

Mix the cubed bread and enough custard to coat the bread, and then some, and let it sit for 10 minutes. Place the bread and custard in a 9-inch or 11-inch square buttered baking dish and cover with the rest of the custard.

Bake in a preheated 350° oven for 30–45 minutes until it is bubbling, the custard is set, and the edges are browned. Serve warm or at room temperature.

We enjoyed this one night at Bacco, a neighborhood Italian restaurant in Mount Pleasant, South Carolina. It was indeed just good food.

Michael Scognamiglio, the owner/chef, was willing to roughly outline the recipe for us. Half the fun was trying to get it just right. Try this recipe and tell us if we figured it out. Unfortunately, Bacco has closed so I'm glad we at least have this recipe.

Easy Fruit Cobbler
serves 8

4 or more cups blueberries, raspberries, strawberries, peaches, apples, or a mixture (the amount depends on the baking pan)
¼–½ cup sugar (depending on the sweetness of the fruit)
1 tablespoon (or a little more) cornstarch to thicken the berries
Squeeze of lemon juice to brighten the fruit flavors

Combine all the ingredients in a bowl. Pour the fruit mixture in a 9 x 9 inch pan, a pie pan, or a cake pan and set aside.

1 cup flour (all-purpose or unbleached)
½ teaspoon kosher salt
¾ cup sugar
8 tablespoons butter (1 stick)

Combine the flour, salt, and sugar and cut the butter into the mixture using a pastry utensil or two knives.

Spread the dough mixture over the fruit and bake at 375° for 45 minutes until the dough is lightly browned. Cool at least 5 minutes and serve with vanilla ice cream.

Cobbler recipes traditionally use a biscuit dough which can be complicated and time consuming. I was introduced to this alternative by my sister-in-law Susan Hoffius. The simplicity immediately won me over.

Susan made it for us with blueberries and strawberries. Two nights later I made it with just strawberries and later with just blueberries. All were outstanding! This is the perfect recipe for what's in season. Even thawed frozen berries will work.

Cream Cheese Pound Cake

serves 8

1½ cups butter (3 sticks), softened
1 8-ounce package cream cheese, softened
3 cups sugar
6 eggs, room temperature
3 cups flour (all-purpose or unbleached) or cake flour (see sidebar)
Dash of kosher salt
1½ teaspoons vanilla extract

Remove the eggs, butter, and cream cheese from the refrigerator an hour or so before getting started.

Preheat oven to 325°. Grease and flour a 10-inch tube or bundt pan. Tap out the extra flour. Cream the butter and the cream cheese. Slowly add the sugar and beat until light and fluffy. Add the eggs, 1 at a time, beating after each addition. Stir in the flour and salt and finally the vanilla.

Pour the batter into the greased pan and level the batter. Bake for 90 minutes, turning the pan at least twice. Cool in the pan for at least 10 minutes. Use a knife to release the sides and invert the pan to place the cake on a plate and then turn the cake right-side up using another plate. Continue cooling on the plate.

Once the cake is cool, dig in. Sliced peaches, strawberries, and even a little ice cream can provide embellishment.

Lemon Glaze: Put 1 cup powdered sugar, 2 tablespoons strained lemon juice, and the zest of 1 lemon in a sauce pan and heat until a sauce is created and pour/brush over the cake. Cool and enjoy!

There are times when a slice of pound cake is the perfect dessert or snack. Fresh strawberries and peaches need a little cake to balance their flavors.

To make cake flour out of all-purpose flour, remove 2 tablespoons from each cup of flour and replace with 2 tablespoons of cornstarch. Necessary? No, but a good variation.

Energy Goodie Balls
serves many

1 cup oatmeal
⅔ cup sweetened flaked coconut
½ cup ground flax seeds
½ cup semi-sweet chocolate chips
½ cup creamy peanut butter
⅓ cup honey, preferably pure, raw, and locally sourced
1 teaspoon vanilla extract

MIx all of the ingredients by hand or spoon and refrigerate. Then roll into balls and keep refrigerated until ready to serve.

One Energy Goodie Ball in the afternoon will make all of the difference to the rest of your day. You may even be willing to share after you finish your first batch!

We had driven 8 hours and arrived at our hosts home, tired and a little spaced out. Our hostess had just made these Energy Goodie Balls. Would I like to try one? As you can see, I did and it was just the boost I needed for the rest of the evening.

They were also great in the car as we headed out the next day. A snack, a picker-upper, and healthy to boot! Don't tell the kids, though, just offer them instead of the cookies or candy they usually reach for.

Ginger Wafers
more than enough

1 cup molasses (Grandma's original unsulphured works great)
½ cup butter (1 stick)
½ cup brown sugar
3¾ cups pastry flour
¾ teaspoon baking soda
¾ teaspoon each ginger, cloves, and cinnamon
½ teaspoon allspice
¼ teaspoon nutmeg

Heat molasses and butter in a sauce pan and stir in the brown sugar. Set aside.

Sift the flour and mix in the spices. Sift again into a large bowl with the molasses mixture, stirring with each sifting until a large ball is created. Refrigerate for at least 3 hours or overnight.

Preheat oven to 375°. Roll half of the dough on a floured board and cut with a round cookie cutter or your favorite. Lightly grease or butter cookie sheets and bake for 8 minutes.

When I was in high school, my family went on a road trip for spring break. Our next-door neighbor gave us a container filled with a version of this cookie. There must have been more than 100 and surprisingly by hoarding them there were a few left when we returned home.

I have been looking for a recipe so that I could recreate the cookies that I remember so fondly. Sixty years later, I found this version and I'm convinced that they are really close!

Lemon Bars
serves 8 generously

½ pound butter (2 sticks)
½ cup powdered sugar
2 cups flour (all-purpose or unbleached), sifted
¼ cup flour with ½ teaspoon baking powder mixed in
2 cups sugar
4 large eggs
¾ cup lemon juice (5–6 lemons), strained, plus the zest of 1 lemon
Extra powdered sugar and extra lemon zest for dusting

Preheat oven to 350°. Blend together the cut-up sticks of butter and the powdered sugar. Mix in the 2 cups of sifted flour. Don't overmix or the resulting crust will be tough. Press the dough in a buttered 9-inch-square baking dish or pan. Bake for 20–25 minutes until the crust is light golden brown. Remove from the oven and set aside.

Combine the eggs, sugar, lemon juice, and flour mixture and pour the filling over the crust. Bake 25–30 minutes. Cool slightly and dust with the extra powdered sugar and grated lemon zest.

Cut into small squares that are easily picked up and eaten in just a bite or two to minimize the powdered sugar falling everywhere.

These are a staple for entertaining. Once your friends have tried them they will make requests. Get the routine down and you will have an easy dish to pass.

While the crust is cooking, you can make the filling. The whole project should take about 1 hour, not including the cooling and sampling.

Paula's Rosemary Shortbread
serves 6-8

1½ cups flour (all-purpose or unbleached)
½ cup cornmeal
⅓ cup sugar
⅓ cup dark brown sugar, packed
1 teaspoon plus a pinch of kosher salt
½ pound cold unsalted butter (2 sticks), cut into pieces
1 tablespoon fresh rosemary, chopped, or 1 teaspoon dried

Preheat oven to 325°. Blend together the flour, cornmeal, sugars, and salt in a food-processor. Add the cut-up butter to the food-processor and pulse to create a grainy mixture. In other words, don't over-pulse!

Press the dough into an unbuttered 9 x 13 inch baking pan. Sprinkle the rosemary on top. Prick the dough with a fork 5 times. Bake for 35 minutes until the crust is light golden brown.

Remove from the oven and immediately cut into small squares with a metal spatula while it is still hot. Leave the shortbread in the pan to cool. Remove and try not to eat too many when no one is looking.

Paula Perlini is a good friend of my wife, June. This is a specialty of hers from her kitchen at Meadowbrook Farm in Lyme, Connecticut. Paula is a renowned interior designer who is also a wonderful cook.

Fortunately for us, she was willing to share this simple but special cookie. Once you have mastered Paula's Rosemary Shortbread, make another batch for your friends!

Blueberry Pecan Galette
serves 8

½ cup toasted pecans
1⅛ cup flour (all-purpose or unbleached)
2 teaspoons sugar
½ teaspoon kosher salt
¼ teaspoon cinnamon
½ cup butter (1 stick), cold, cut-up into pieces

Preheat oven to 375°. Pulse the pecans in a food processor to a coarse meal, then add the flour, sugar, salt, and cinnamon and pulse to combine. Add butter and pulse until the mixture becomes a coarse meal. Transfer the mixture to a bowl and drizzle with about 4 tablespoons of ice water so that the mixture comes together. Form into a 6-inch disk and chill in plastic wrap for at least 1 hour. You can hold the dough in the refrigerator for up to 2 days before completing the galette.

Filling:
12 ounces blueberries (about 2 cups)
2 teaspoons strained lemon juice
1½ tablespoons cornstarch
¼ teaspoon kosher salt
¼ cup sugar (plus extra for sprinkling on top before baking)

Roll dough on a lightly floured surface into a 12-inch oval, then transfer to a parchment-lined rimmed baking sheet. Combine the blueberries and lemon juice in a bowl and mix with the cornstarch, salt, and sugar. Mound the blueberries on the dough and fold the edges over. Brush the edges with milk and sprinkle with sugar. Bake until the galette is golden brown and the filling is bubbling. Cool and serve.

When blueberries are fresh, it's nice to have multiple go-to recipes, so you don't tire of having the same dish. This recipe will make a great addition to your rotation.

This recipe also works well with frozen blueberries. To freeze blueberries, don't wash them, just place them on a rimmed cookie sheet to freeze. After they're frozen put them in freezer bags and return to freezer. Wash the blueberries before use.

Plum Torte
serves 8

¼ pound butter (1 stick), softened, cut into pieces
1 cup sugar
2 large eggs
1 cup flour (all-purpose or unbleached), sifted
1 teaspoon baking powder
Dash of kosher salt
24 purple plums, halved and pitted
2 tablespoons sugar, ½ teaspoon cinnamon, and 1 tablespoon lemon zest for dusting

Preheat oven to 350°. Blend together the cut-up stick of butter and the sugar until they are creamed. Mix in the eggs one at a time. Meanwhile add the baking powder and a dash of salt to the flour and sift into the creamed mixture. Stir the flour into the creamed mixture until combined.

Spoon the batter into a buttered springform cake pan of 8 to 10 inches. Place the plum halves skin-side up on top of the batter across the pan. Mix the lemon zest into the cinnamon sugar and sprinkle on top. Bake approximately 1 hour until the cake top is golden and cooked through. Serve plain or with whipped cream or vanilla ice cream.

Alternative: Replace ¼ cup of the sugar with light or dark brown sugar. Add 1 more egg, 1 tablespoon lemon zest, 1 teaspoon vanilla extract, and ½ teaspoon nutmeg. In place of the plums use approximately 4 cups of blueberries, raspberries, blackberries, peaches, or a mixture. This will be more like a buckle and may collapse into a cake of goodness. Cook just a little less for a more moist, pudding-like cake.

Ease and speed of this creation makes it a summer staple. It can be made at the last minute and the smells as your guests arrive will make the dinner a success before a fork is lifted. The warm torte after dinner will be the final hit!

This recipe and its variation comes from the New York Times *and was its most requested recipe over the years after it was published in 1983. I told several friends who like to cook about it, and they all had made it. They too praised its simplicity.*

Butterscotch Sauce
serves 8

6 tablespoons butter, cut into pieces
¼ cup heavy cream or whipping cream
¾ cup light brown sugar
Pinch of kosher salt

Melt the butter in a saucepan and add the cream, cooking over low to medium heat, stirring. Add the brown sugar and salt and continue to stir until the sauce starts to thicken, 5–10 minutes, depending on how high your heat is.

Cool and serve on ice cream, cake, or coffee cake. Refrigerate and slightly reheat as necessary.

You have vanilla ice cream in the freezer but no fresh strawberries, peaches, or blueberries to put on it. Look at these ingredients, you probably have them. All you need is 10-15 minutes.

If you make one of them just before dinner, everyone will rave that the sauce is warm!

Chocolate Sauce

4 ounces semi-sweet or bittersweet chocolate (not unsweetened)
¼ cup sugar
½ cup heavy cream or whipping cream
¼ teaspoon kosher salt
1 teaspoon vanilla extract

Melt the chocolate in a nonreactive saucepan and add the remaining ingredients in the order listed, stirring until it is all dissolved. Refrigerate until ready to serve over ice cream.

Vanilla Ice Cream
serves 8

Ice cream maker
1 cup whole milk
1½ ounces (3 tablespoons) cream cheese
¾ cup sugar
2 cups heavy cream or whipping cream
1 tablespoon vanilla extract
½ teaspoon kosher salt

Heat the milk and cream cheese in a nonreactive (stainless steel) saucepan. Add the sugar and stir until the sugar is dissolved. Remove from the heat and add the cream, vanilla extract, and salt and stir. Refrigerate overnight or at least 3 hours.

Strain the cream mixture into the ice cream maker and process until firm but not hard, about 15 minutes. Remove from the ice cream maker and freeze at least 15 minutes before serving. Serve with pie, crisp, or brownies, and/or a little Chocolate Sauce (recipe on previous page).

Objective: a foolproof vanilla ice cream that can be made quickly to impress your friends. It works!

The challenge here was to make a rich ice cream without egg yolks that require special attention to avoid curdling.

To make it chocolate ice cream, melt 4 ounces of semi-sweet or bittersweet chocolate in the sauce pan and add the sugar before the milk and cream cheese.

Hot Chocolate
serves 1

2 heaping teaspoons sugar
1 heaping teaspoon cocoa
¼ teaspoon vanilla extract
Dash of cinnamon
1 cup milk, preferably whole milk for a richer cup of hot chocolate

Saucepan:
Mix the first four ingredients in a saucepan. Add a little milk and stir until you have a sauce. Add the remaining milk and stir until it looks like chocolate milk. Continue cooking over medium heat until it reaches serving temperature.

Microwave:
Mix the first four ingredients in a cup. Stir in the milk. Heat for 45 seconds and stir, repeat and serve!

Instant Alternative:
Make your own container of instant hot chocolate by using 5 cups dry milk powder, 2½ cups confectioners sugar, 1 cup cocoa powder, and 1 cup non-dairy creamer. Add ingredients to a bowl and mix with a large spoon. Store in an airtight container until you are ready. Add ⅓ cup of the mixture to a coffee cup with 1 cup of boiling water (or follow the above instructions with milk).

On a cold winter afternoon there is nothing more restorative than a cup of hot chocolate. This may become a ritual.

If you only make 1 cup, you may find others eyeing you with longing expressions. To serve 4, use 1 heaping tablespoon for the first two ingredients, 1 teaspoon vanilla extract, ¼ teaspoon cinnamon, and 4 cups of milk.

If the instant alternative isn't chocolaty enough, you can use up to 2 cups of cocoa. Add ¼ cup at a time and test with a little hot water.

Acknowledgments

Acknowledgments

Writing my first cookbook was actually a fairly short effort. Most of the recipes were already gathered in my handwritten three-ring binder. The task was to convert them into a publishable form.

In 2008 Apple provided One to One coaching in one-hour increments each week in their Apple stores. The charge was $99 for the year. Meanwhile, my brother Steve was an accomplished editor who could provide both moral and technical support. The result was that *Just Good Food* was completed and published in 2009, after just two years (and a lifetime of cooking and gathering recipes).

This second cookbook has been much more challenging. I had almost no recipes after the first book, so I had to start gathering recipes once again. The most common question as I promoted the first book was, "Are you working on a sequel?" Eventually, I was. Very slowly.

Almost five years after the first cookbook was published, my wife of almost forty-five years, Vickie, died. I had to find myself and find June, my new bride, who had written two cookbooks in a surprisingly similar style for holiday gifts. We married in 2017 and I had a new tester and critic. Now what to do with that second cookbook?

Meanwhile, Apple ended One to One service and my computer got out of date, but I kept plugging away. No end in sight! I needed real support as I was unable to master Apple Support on the phone. An updated team was necessary: brother Steve and James Cantrill, the son of a lifelong cottage friend, Margaret ("Boo") Johnston. All it took was patience and smarts, commonly referred to as technical expertise. In other words, this would never have been completed without Steve and James and my testers, primarily guests at the cottage, and most especially June!

Recipes came from magazines, newspapers, cookbooks, and friends, but they all had to be tested and simplified to fit the *Just Good Food* philosophy. Yes, there is a philosophy. I wish I could explain why some recipes fit and others didn't. They just did.

Now the hope is that you enjoy it, and actually cook from it. Thank you for trying!

Index

Almond Biscotti, 102
Appetizers:
    Asparagus Wrapped in Bread, 9
    Asparagus Wrapped in Prosciutto, 9
    Avocado Tomato Salsa, 12
    Blue Cheese Dip, 5, 6
    Bread and Butter Pickles, 19
    Cajun Dip, 6
    Caramelized Onion Relish, 16
    Charleston Cheese, 2
    Cheese Puffs, 4
    Cheese Straws, 3
    Crostini, 11
    Curry Dip, 7
    Deviled Eggs, 104
    Herb Cream Cheese, 15
    Hummus with Thyme, 8
    Meatloaf Paté, 10
    Mexican Salsa (with Shrimp), 13
    Mushroom and Onion Bruschetta, 17
    Oven-baked Chicken Wings, 76
    Pickled Asparagus, 18
    Queso Dip, 6
    Salsa Verde, 14
    Whitefish Spread, 11
Asparagus:
    Asparagus Soup, 30
    Pickled Asparagus, 18
    Wrapped in Bread, 9
    Wrapped in Prosciutto, 9
Assistance:
    Lena Chamberlain, 128
    Barbara Hoffius, 25
    June Bowman Hoffius, 1–140
    Susan Hoffius, 130
    David Niven, 79
    Paula Perlini, 79, 135
    Michael Scognamiglio, 129
    Fred Sytsma, 122
    Barb Verhage, 12
Avocado Toast, 123
Avocado Tomato Salsa, 12
Baking Powder, 115
Barbecue Sauce, 61
Beans: Tuscan White Beans, 50
Beef:
    Beef and Mushroom Pasta, 100
    Beef Bourguignon, 64
    Beef Brisket Sandwiches, 122
    Beef or Pork Stir Fry, 68
    Beef Stroganoff, 65
    Ground Beef Tacos, 72
    Peppered Steak in Beer & Garlic, 66
    Short Ribs and Swiss Chard, 67
Beef and Mushroom Pasta, 100
Beef Bourguignon, 64
Beef Brisket Sandwiches, 122
Beef or Pork Stir Fry, 68
Beef Stroganoff, 65
Biscuits, 115
Black Bean Chili, 31
Blue Cheese Dip, 5, 6
Blueberry Cornmeal Coffee Cake, 117
Blueberry Pecan Galette, 136
Bread and Butter Pickles, 19
Bread Pudding, Panettone, 129
Bread: French Toast, 109
Breads:
    Biscuits, 115
    Blueberry Cornmeal Coffee Cake, 117
    Cranberry Nut Bread, 116
    Croutons, 23

Hot French Bread with Herbs, 114
Breakfast Hash, 108
Breakfast. *See* Brunch
Broiled Fish, 85
Brownies, Double Chocolate, 126
Brunch:
    Almond Biscotti, 102
    Biscuits, 115
    Blueberry Cornmeal Coffee Cake, 117
    Breakfast Hash, 108
    Cheese Soufflé, 110
    Cranberry Nut Bread, 116
    French Toast, 109
    Granola, 103
    Johnnycakes, 112
    Mess for Breakfast, A, 106
    Sausage Gravy, 105
    Sour Cream Pancakes, 111
    Tomato and Cheese Frittata, 107
Brussels Sprouts, 42
Buffalo Chicken Wings. *See* Oven-baked
    Chicken Wings, 76
Butterflied Chicken, 77
Buttermilk Salad Dressing, 22
Butterscotch Sauce, 138
Caesar Salad, Simple, 23
Cajun Dip, 6
Cake flour, 131
Caramelized Onion Relish, 16
Cauliflower, Roasted, 41
Cauliflower Steak, 41
Cereal: Granola, 103
Charleston Cheese, 2
Cheese:
    Blue Cheese Dip, 5, 6
    Charleston Cheese, 2
    Cheese Puffs, 4

    Cheese Soufflé, 110
    Cheese Straws, 3
    Herb Cream Cheese, 15
    Queso Dip, 6
Cheese Puffs, 4
Cheese Soufflé, 110
Cheese Straws, 3
Chicken:
    Butterflied Chicken, 77
    Chicken á la King, 80
    Chicken Noodle Soup, 32
    Chicken Parmesan, 97
    Chicken Salad Sandwiches, 120
    Oven-baked Chicken Wings, 76
    Roast Lemon Chicken, 79
    Saltimbocca Chicken, 82
    Simply Baked Chicken, 78
    Skillet Chicken, 81
Chicken á la King, 80
Chicken Noodle Soup, 32
Chicken Parmesan, 97
Chicken Salad Sandwiches, 120
Chili, Black Bean, 31
Chocolate Ice Cream, 139
Chocolate Sauce, 138
Cioppino – Fish Stew, 34
Cod, Boursin Cheese, and Tomatoes, 92
Cole Slaw, 86
Comeback Sauce, 59
Cookies: Ginger Wafers, 133
Coquilles St. Jacques, 90
Cranberry Ketchup, 62
Cranberry Nut Bread, 116
Cream Cheese Pound Cake, 131
Creamed Fresh Spinach, 43
Crostini, 11
Croutons, 23

Curry Dip, 7
Desserts:
    Blueberry Pecan Galette, 136
    Butterscotch Sauce, 138
    Cake flour, 131
    Chocolate Ice Cream, 139
    Chocolate Sauce, 138
    Cream Cheese Pound Cake, 131
    Double Chocolate Brownies, 126
    Double Chocolate Pudding, 127
    Energy Goodie Bars, 132
    Ginger Wafers, 133
    Hot Chocolate, 140
    Lemon Bars, 134
    Lemon Glaze, 131
    Panettone Bread Pudding, 129
    Paula's Rosemary Shortbread, 135
    Plum Torte, 137
    Strawberry Shortcake, 128
    Vanilla Ice Cream, 139
Deviled Eggs, 104
Dips:
    Blue Cheese Dip, 5, 6
    Cajun Dip, 6
    Curry Dip, 7
    Hummus with Thyme, 8
    Queso Dip, 6
Double Chocolate Brownies, 126
Double Chocolate Pudding, 127
Easy Fruit Cobbler, 130
Egg Salad Sandwiches, 118
Eggplant Parmesan, 97
Eggs:
    Cheese Soufflé, 110
    Deviled Eggs, 104
    Egg Salad Sandwiches, 118

    Hardboiled Eggs, 118
Energy Goodie Bars, 132
English Pea Soup, 37
Fennel, Roasted, 46
Fish Stew (Cioppino), 34
Fish Tacos and Slaw, 86
Fishcakes, 87
Flank Steak, Marinades for, 56
French Bread, Hot, with Herbs, 114
French Potato Salad, 27
French Toast, 109
Frogmore Stew, 33
Fruit Cobbler, Easy, 130
Fruit Torte, 137
Fruits:
    Blueberry Cornmeal Coffee Cake, 117
    Blueberry Pecan Galette, 136
    Blueberries, frozen, 136
    Cranberry Ketchup, 62
    Cranberry Nut Bread, 116
    Easy Fruit Cobbler, 130
    Fruit Torte, 137
    Lemon Bars, 134
    Lemon Glaze, 131
    Plum Torte, 137
    Strawberry Shortcake, 128
Ginger Wafers, 133
Granola, 103
Grilled Fish, 85
Hardboiled Eggs, 118
Hasselback Potato Gratin, 49
Herb Cream Cheese, 15
Hoppin' John, 52
Hot Chocolate, 140
Hot Dogs: Mexi Chili Dogs, 121
Hummus with Thyme, 8

Ice Cream:
    Chocolate, 139
    Vanilla, 139
Johnnycakes, 112
Ketchup, Cranberry, 62
Lamb Shanks, 74
Lamb:
    Lamb Shanks, 74
    Rack of Lamb, 73
Leaping Frog Chicken. *See* Butterflied Chicken, 77
Lemon Bars, 134
Lemon Glaze, 131
Lentil Salad, Moroccan, 24
Lobster Rolls, 88
Lobster Tails, 88
Marinade for Rack of Lamb, 73
Marinades for Flank Steak, 56
Meatloaf Paté, 10
Mess for Breakfast, A, 106
Mexi Chili Dogs, 121
Mexican Salsa (with Shrimp), 13
Moroccan Lentil Salad, 24
Mushroom and Onion Bruschetta, 17
Mussels in White Wine, 84
Mustard Sauce, 61
Mustard, Whole Grain, 60
Onion:
    Caramelized Onion Relish, 16
    Mushroom and Onion Bruschetta, 17
    Pickled Red Onions, 20
Oven-baked Chicken Wings, 76
Panettone Bread Pudding, 129
Pasta:
    Beef and Mushroom Pasta, 100
    Pasta Carbonara, 94
    Pasta Primavera, 95
    Pesto Sauce, 96
    Shrimp and Caper Pasta, 98
Pasta Carbonara, 94
Pasta Primavera, 95
Pate: Meatloaf Paté, 10
Paula's Rosemary Shortbread, 135
Pea, English, Soup, 37
Peppered Steak in Beer & Garlic, 66
Pesto Sauce, 96
Philly Sandwich, 124
Pickled Asparagus, 18
Pickled Red Onions, 20
Pickles:
    Bread and Butter Pickles, 19
    Pickled Asparagus, 18
    Pickled Red Onions, 20
Plum Torte, 137
Pork Chops in Lemon Caper Sauce, 70
Pork Medallions in Mushroom Wine Sauce, 71
Pork:
    Beef or Pork Stir Fry, 68
    Pork Chops in Lemon Caper Sauce, 70
    Pork Medallions in Mushroom Wine Sauce, 71
    Pork Tacos, 72
Pork Tacos, 72
Potato Salad, French, 27
Potato Salad, Summer, 28
Potatoes:
    French Potato Salad, 27
    Hasselback Potato Gratin, 49
    Roasted Sweet Potato Fries, 51
    Summer Potato Salad, 28
    Twice-Baked Potato Casserole, 48
Pound Cake, Cream Cheese, 131
Prosciutto, Asparagus Wrapped in, 9
Pudding, Double Chocolate, 127

Pudding, Panettone Bread, 129
Queso Dip, 6
Rack of Lamb, 73
Rattlesnake Salt, 55
Ravigole Sauce, 57
Risotto, Shrimp and Sausage, 99
Roast Lemon Chicken, 79
Roasted Cauliflower, 41
Roasted Fennel, 46
Roasted Sweet Potato Fries, 51
Salad Dressings: Buttermilk Salad Dressing, 22
Salad Nicoise, 26
Salads:
    Caesar Salad, Simple, 23
    Chicken Salad, 120
    Cole Slaw, 86
    Egg Salad, 118
    French Potato Salad, 27
    Moroccan Lentil Salad, 24
    Salad Nicoise, 26
    Summer Potato Salad, 28
    Tuna Salad, 119
    Wilted Salad, 25
Salmon in Parchment, 91
Salsa Verde, Fresh, 14
Salsa:
    Avocado Tomato Salsa, 12
    Fresh Salsa Verde, Fresh, 14
    Mexican Salsa (with Shrimp), 13
Saltimbocca Chicken, 82
Salts and Spices:
    Comeback Sauce, 59
    Cranberry Ketchup, 62
    Marinades for Flank Steak, 56
    Mustard Sauce, 61
    Mustard, Whole Grain, 60

    Rattlesnake Salt, 55
    Ravigole Sauce, 57
    Savory Grilling Rub, 69
    Thyme for Salt, 54
    Tuscan Rosemary Salt, 55
    Worcestershire Sauce, Fresh, 58
Sandwiches:
    Avocado Toast, 123
    Beef Brisket Sandwiches, 122
    Chicken Salad Sandwiches, 120
    Egg Salad Sandwiches, 118
    Mexi Chili Dogs, 121
    Philly Sandwich, 124
    Tuna Salad Sandwiches, 119
Sausage Gravy, 55, 105
Sausage, and Shrimp, Risotto, 99
Sautéed Fish, 85
Savory Grilling Rub, 69
Scallops. *See* Coquilles St. Jacques, 90
Seafood:
    Broiled Fish, 85
    Cioppino – Fish Stew, 34
    Cod, Boursin Cheese, and Tomatoes, 92
    Coquilles St. Jacques, 90
    Fish Tacos and Slaw, 86
    Fishcakes, 87
    Grilled Fish, 85
    Lobster Tails, 88
    Mexican Salsa (with Shrimp), 13
    Mussels in White Wine, 84
    Salad Nicoise, 26
    Salmon in Parchment, 91
    Sautéed Fish, 85
    Shrimp and Caper Pasta, 98
    Shrimp and Grits, 89
    Shrimp and Sausage Risotto, 99

Shrimp Chowder, 35
Tuna Salad Sandwiches, 119
Whitefish Spread, 11
Sesame Snow Peas, 45
Short Ribs and Swiss Chard, 67
Shortbread, Paula's Rosemary, 135
Shortcake, Strawberry, 128
Shrimp and Caper Pasta, 98
Shrimp and Grits, 89
Shrimp and Sausage Risotto, 99
Shrimp Chowder, 35
Side Dishes:
    Hasselback Potato Gratin, 49
    Hoppin' John, 52
    Roasted Sweet Potato Fries, 51
    Tuscan White Beans, 50
    Twice Baked Potato Casserole, 48
Simple Caesar Salad, 23
Simply Baked Chicken, 78
Skillet Chicken, 81
Snow Peas, 45
Soup:
    Chicken Noodle Soup, 32
    Asparagus Soup, page 30
    Black Bean Chili, 31
    Cioppino – Fish Stew, 34
    English Pea Soup, 37
    Frogmore Stew, 33
    Shrimp Chowder, 35
    Tomato Bisque with Fresh Goat Cheese, 36
    Workout Potassium Soup, 38
Sour Cream Pancakes, 111
Spatchcock Chicken. See Butterflied Chicken, 77
Spinach, Creamed Fresh, 43
Stir Fry: Beef / Pork, 68
Strawberry Shortcake, 128
Summer Potato Salad, 28
Sweet Potatoes: Roasted Sweet Potato Fries, 51
Swiss Chard, 44

Swiss Chard: Short Ribs and Swiss Chard, 67
Tacos:
    Fish Tacos and Slaw, 86
    Ground Beef, 72
    Pork, 72
Thyme for Salt, 54
Tomato and Cheese Frittata, 107
Tomato Bisque with Fresh Goat Cheese, 36
Torte, Plum, 137
Tuna: Salad Nicoise, 26
Tuna Salad Sandwiches, 119
Turkey á la King, 80
Tuscan Rosemary Salt, 55
Tuscan White Beans, 50
Twice-Baked Potato Casserole, 48
Vanilla Ice Cream, 139
Vegetables:
    Asparagus Soup, 30
    Beef / Pork Stir Fry, 68
    Cauliflower Steak, 41
    Cole Slaw, 86
    Creamed Fresh Spinach, 43
    Eggplant Parmesan, 97
    Glazed Brussels Sprouts, 42
    Moroccan Lentil Salad, 24
    Pickled Asparagus, 18
    Roasted Cauliflower, 41
    Roasted Fennel, 46
    Sesame Snow Peas, 45
    Snow Peas, 45
    Swiss Chard, 44
    Tuscan White Beans, 50
    Zucchini Gratin, 40
Whitefish Spread, 11
Whole Grain Mustard, 60
Wilted Salad, 25
Worcestershire Sauce, Fresh, 58
Workout Potassium Soup, 38
Zucchini Gratin, 40

About the Author

Dirk Hoffius published *Just Good Food for good friends* in 2009, and has been cooking and collecting additional recipes ever since. He has been an estate-planning attorney at Varnum, Riddering, Schmidt & Howlett in Grand Rapids, Michigan, for over 50 years. A determined booster of Grand Rapids, he has served and supported more community nonprofits than he can count. He is a graduate of Colgate University and the University of Virginia Law School.

He and his wife, the former June Bowman, divide their time between Grand Rapids, their cottage at Point Nipigon on the Straits of Mackinac, and a home in Palm Desert, California.